19 RESIDENCES IN 19 YEARS OF HELL AND HUMOR

19 RESIDENCES
IN 19 YEARS OF
HELL AND HUMOR

❧

Fred W. Campbell

WESTBOW
PRESS
A DIVISION OF THOMAS NELSON

WestBow Press books may be ordered through booksellers or by contacting:

WestBow Press
A Division of Thomas Nelson
1663 Liberty Drive
Bloomington, IN 47403
www.westbowpress.com
1-(866) 928-1240

Because of the dynamic nature of the Internet, any Web addresses or links contained in this book may have changed since publication and may no longer be valid. The views expressed in this work are solely those of the author and do not necessarily reflect the views of the publisher, and the publisher hereby disclaims any responsibility for them.

ISBN: 978-1-4497-0520-6 (sc)
ISBN: 978-1-4497-0521-3 (dj)
ISBN: 978-1-4497-0519-0 (e)

Library of Congress Control Number: 2010935756

Printed in the United States of America

WestBow Press rev. date: 12/13/2010

Dedications

I dedicate this book to each and every one of the hard working people that made it through the depression, the people who had the will to go and make their lives for their selves, which was much better than their childhood.

I also dedicate this book to my brothers and sisters, because we all lived through the same conditions.

I also dedicate this book to my wife and two children. They were all there with me every time I needed them, the most. Their prayers, support and with God's help made it possible for me to be alive after open heart surgery and a pace maker installed. My family made me stronger and knowing that God was there for me, made me even stronger yet. May God Bless All. I thank everyone for their love and support.

CONTENTS

Prologue

This story is true. The story is about a family that got started in the depression. This is written by the second sibling in the family. This is a story of how the second child, born into the family, saw hunger, hard times, hard work, fun, laughing, and happiness of a poor family. We all struggled to make it on a daily basis. Sometimes fighting and protecting ourselves came into play when it came our way.

I've tried to write this book where anyone can read it. The young, the old, the middle aged or whomever. I'm writing this book the only way I know how to write. I finished High School with a general education and self taught for the rest of what I know. Enjoy the reading and hope there is some humor here and there as it was for me.

If you think you know what is rough, just wait until you read this book. When someone says they had it bad, do some comparing with them, and let them know what a wonderful life they had.

Chapter 1

Maplewood Avenue

It all started for me in 1939, when I was born into a poor family of three—my father, mother, and older brother. It was during the depression, and most people were poor. The depression had started in 1929, and the end was in sight when the war came about. There were very few jobs, and the pay was not much. People had to do whatever they could to keep food on the table. Very few jobs provided the food, shelter, clothing, and other necessities of life that a family needed during this period of time. Times were hard, but people adapted to the hardships and sacrifices were made by different members of a family in order to survive.

Neither of my parents had a education; Dad had gone through three grades, and Mom had six grades. This meant that my parents were labor people and farmers, as you will find out later. Most of the time when farming, it was sharecropping. The depression was in effect for ten years, and then came the war. I started remembering things very clearly at five years old. I cannot remember when Hawaii was bombed. I do remember almost starving to death with my mother and brother. I remember this old house on Maplewood Avenue in Tullahoma, Tennessee. I remember the old grocery store where my mom had a charge account. When the credit was exhausted, Mrs. Scott, the store owner, had to cut us off—and everyone else too, because she could not extend credit any longer.

We had moved three times already since my birth. This was the fourth place we lived, and I do not remember the other places. This is the best I can figure out from my mom. Mom is ninety-three years and six months old at this writing. Things are slipping now. She has been living for over fifty years with one kidney. She is in pretty good health and eating well, but her mind shows signs of giving up: it comes and goes. My youngest brother told me that he had visited my mom recently. He said that when he and his wife walked in, my mom got up and packed her bags. Then she said, "I am ready to go home." My brother got her to take a nap, and they slipped out and left my mom sleeping.

My Dad & Mom, oldest Brother on Left and I'm on the Right.

When the war began, my father said, "I'm joining the army to serve my country." Telling this to my mom did not go over too well. But after my father explained what he had in mind, it started to make sense and my mother bought it. My father had said, "It means a job and earning money for the family and serving the country at the same time."

While talking to Mom about this recently, I asked her if she thought he would be coming back. Mom said, "I didn't know what to think. Your father had done some crazy things since we were married."

"Like what?" I asked.

Mom said, "Your father was working at a nursery three or four days a week, and that was it. I was ironing clothes and doing some housecleaning part-time wherever I could find it. I ordered some shoes from the Sears Roebuck catalog. When the shoes came in, the bill came with them. I put the money in an envelope and gave it to your dad, saying, 'Since you are going through town, mail this letter for me.' He asked what it was, and I told him, 'That is money to pay for the boys' shoes.' He said okay and was off to make his rounds. When he got home, he was drunk."

My dad never said a word about mailing the letter, and Mom had no reason to ask. A week went by, and a man from Sears Roebuck came by and said he wanted the money for the shoes or the shoes. Mom said she had no money. She set us boys down, pulled off the shoes, and gave them to him.

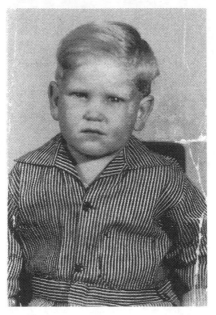

This is me at Age 2 ½ years old

So my father went off to war to serve his country. He joined the army. The army put him in the army engineers, which at that time meant being a carpenter, building anything that needed building.

Then came the orders to go to Hawaii for a two-year tour and help build Hawaii back to the way it used to be. From the time he joined up, it took three and a half months for the first check to get to my mother. I remember very well what was going on in our lives during this time. Hunger must have got my mind into working order, because I remember almost starving to death. Credit was overextended at the grocery store. Cornmeal gravy, corn cakes, or flapjacks—that was the full menu at our house for quite a spell. I can remember my mother going to her best friend and neighbor wanting to borrow some fatback or bacon grease so she could keep frying the flapjacks and making the gravy. Our friend gave her the grease and said, "We pour out all we don't use

for our gravy. You are welcome to it, and I will save it for you."
Our neighbor became one of my best friends after that.

This is my oldest Brother at Age 5 and me, at age 3

Times were hard for everyone at that time, and most people
had to do whatever they could to survive. Winter came, and we
finally got the checks coming in from the government. We burned
coal for heat and cooking. All the homes had coal or wood bins
to store their coal or wood in. Some people knew that we had a
regular check coming in, and others could see the smoke coming
from the fire. This meant we had purchased at least two tons
of coal or more for winter warmth. Thieves would come in the
middle of the night or early morning and steal our coal. We had
to stay up as late as we could with a big club for protection. This
did not work. We put tin cans on strings that would make loud
noises when they were moved. Then my mother loosened some
of the boards near the coal bin by pulling out some of the nails.
When stepped on, the board would rise up and make noise. One
of these boards must have done more than that because there was
a loud noise and the cans started rattling and making even more
noise. My mother, being a light sleeper, had heard most of the

noise and shouted, "Get up, Pop, and get the gun." Grunts came from the back porch, and then all was quiet. My mother while waking up must have been thinking she was at home with her family and called for her papa, who always had an old shotgun for protection and hunting purposes.

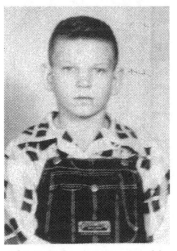

This is me at Age 8 years old.

The next day the neighbors and my mother were talking about the noise that happened the night before. Everyone speculated on what had happened. Finally all agreed that the board must have been stepped on at the very end and must have hit the man in the face, forcing him to fall into the strings of tin cans, making all the noise. The string and the cans were strung out and lead down the back toward the backyard. Word must have gotten out that we had a gun, because the stealing stopped. We made it through the winter with the coal we had left.

Before the government check started coming in, the radio was blasting the news of the war. Very little did I understand about it. My family and I were having a rough time of it. My mother tried to find some paying work to do, but she had no success.

The radio had the answer to the problem. The newsman said that America needed all of the scrap metal brought in and good money would be paid for it. He said tin cans, iron, steel, or anything of metal was needed. We lived just on the edge of town. Between us and the town, there were woods with several scattered piles of cans. We had a little red wagon, and Mom instantly knew what we were going to do. We were going to pick up tin cans and sell them for money.

The next morning we three—my mother, brother, and I—were off to find tin cans. We picked up and crushed the cans so we could haul a big load. We also brought along some toe sacks to fill up with the tin cans. I, being the youngest, went after the shiny new cans first. We cleaned up all the cans that we could on the top surface and found out that there were more under the leaves. So the following day we brought along a garden hoe and pulled the cans loose from under the decaying leaves. We cleared out all the woods and looked for other places to find tin cans. Mom would stay home to catch up on the housework; my brother and I knew what to do and where to go. We rounded up every tin can that we could that was in our range of walking distance. Then everyone caught on to what we doing, and the tin can business were dried up. The money from the tin can sales and the fat grease from our neighbor provided enough food to last until the government checks started coming in. It's hard looking back on it now, but then I was so young, only five and a half years old. It must have seemed like fun to me then because I don't remember getting tired.

I started school in the fall, and I was on top of the world. I was learning new things and seeing new things that I had never come in contact with before. New foods were first, then came pencils and paper—and a pencil sharpener that was hand cranked. Boy, what a sharp point! Then came the paddle, handled by the biggest principal that I had ever seen—in fact, the only one that I had ever seen. We had a substitute teacher one day; I cannot remember her name. My regular teacher was out sick. Miss Campbell was my regular teacher's name. My teacher knew there was no kinship between us. My teacher never said anything about it, and I was so young at this time I did not know what it meant anyway. Looking back, I know for sure the teacher did not want to lay claim to kinship.

Then it happened. A class bully came by my desk after sharpening his pencil and rammed the pencil into my arm. The point broke off in my arm. I pulled the lead out and got up from my desk without saying a word or crying. I started sharpening my pencil and got a great point on it. The bully was watching, so I went and sat back down at my desk. When everything was quiet and he had forgotten about watching me, I acted. I went over to him walking up from behind and stabbed him in the same place where he had stabbed me. He screamed out really loud, and the kids went running to the front of the room. The bully was crying and screaming, and the substitute teacher was turning white and hanging onto her desk. I calmly went back to my desk and sat down again.

When the teacher got her composure back and the color returned to her face, she went to see about the bully. He told his side of the story and left out the most important part—that he had started it by stabbing me first with his pencil. After she found out he was not going to die and the blood would wipe off leaving a hole in his arm that would heal given time, the teacher came over to my desk. With no questions asked, she grabbed me by the arm and said, "You are going to the office and get a paddling." But what the substitute teacher did not know was how hard it was going to be to get me out of the desk. She pulled, but I did not move. Then she started asking for help. I had my legs wrapped around the desk legs and was holding on with my hands. The teacher asked for one, then two, and then three boys to help her. Working together, they got me loose from the desk and were pulling me toward the office. When I got to the office and saw the huge principal, I quit struggling and stood still. The teacher told the bully's story, and my pants were set on fire. I was told to stand in the hallway until my eyes dried up and then go and wash my face and return to the classroom

I could not wait to get home where I could tell my mom what had taken place that day at school. I explained what had happened and showed my arm to my mom. Mom got mad as you know what. The next morning Mom and I walked to school together, and straight to the principal's office we went. My mom was explaining but getting nowhere until she told me to show the principal my arm. My mom asked, "Did you ask him for his side of the story? No, you did not, nor did the teacher.

The principal said, "If he had only cried out, that would have given us a reason to look at his arm. Then we would have gotten his side of the story."

Mom told the principal that we were being taught not to look for trouble, but to fight back whenever it came our way. The principal's apology was accepted by my mom, and it was all right with me too. I could feel that my skin was different—harder and smoother for some reason, but it did not hurt anymore.

Chapter 2

Georgia Bound

This is my oldest Brother on Right and me again at some old farm, no one in family remembers where or when

Through letters my dad let Mom know he wanted us to move to Georgia and live near his sister while he was in the army. So to Georgia we went, but it did not last long. Aunt Abbey wanted my mom to give the government check to her. Aunt Abbey said she would pay the bills and buy the food and manage the money until my dad came home from the army. I think you know what happened then: Mom went unglued and told Aunt Abbey to get out, that she could manage the money just fine without her help. My mom wrote my grandpa, who could not read or write and had to take the letter to the grocery store to get it read for him. Mom asked Grandpa to come and live with us until she saved up the money for the move back to Tullahoma, Tennessee.

I can remember Grandpa sitting on the front porch in a straight-back chair with his back propped up against the wall. My brother and I would slip up and tickle his nose with a feather while he was dozing in the sunshine. We kids knew that Grandpa would not take much fooling around before he would bust our bottoms. We kids had a getaway plan. There was a dirt bank to slide down from the yard to the road. The bank was about thirty feet long from the top to the bottom and was on a fairly gentle incline. I could run and hit the slide area, dropping to my bottom. I could slide down to the road and run to the house and hide until Grandpa cooled off.

Our plan was a great one, we thought. We started our agitating again, Grandpa jumped up, and we ran off and down the slide. We looked for Grandpa to be behind us, but he was not. We finally saw Grandpa over by the trees cutting a switch. He went back and sat down on the porch again in the same position and leaned back against the wall. My older brother and I talked it over, and we decided to start the agitation once again. With Grandpa's eyes closed, this was easy, we thought. Up to that time, we did not know that Grandpa could run—and fast. But we soon found out. Chicken feather in hand, nose tickling was fun. All of a sudden, Grandpa jumped up, and the switch was making a noise we had not heard before. It was hitting us! Swish. Then it would hit again—swish—and we were running as fast as we could run. We looked behind us, and Grandpa was right there. We hit the slide area on the run, the two of us brothers and then Grandpa, down the slide all three of us, as if we were on a bobsled. At the bottom Grandpa grabbed both of us and started to the house. We knew what was coming, but it did not happen. Grandpa sat us down on the porch and gave us a good talking-to, shaking the switch occasionally. We got to the point where we did not bother him anymore while he was napping.

We asked all kinds of questions: how did he learn to run so fast and how did he know how to slide down a hill. Then Grandpa told us about the moonshine days. Grandpa said they were living around Winchester, and their sheriff was named George. The sheriff was known as the fastest man around any of the local towns. The sheriff would run down a moonshiner and arrest him. The sheriff wanted someone to take off running so he could have a footrace. Grandpa said, "Well, kids, he got his race. We were making moonshine over at the foot of the mountain. When the call came, revenuers and everyone started to scramble, running in all directions. It was wintertime, and I was wearing an overcoat with long tails. I looked over my shoulder and saw the sheriff had picked me out to run down. I was running along the ridge and had to jump a fence. Landing on my feet, I looked back and saw the sheriff had cleared the fence too. I knew that after jumping the fence, I had to keep going down the ridge to the bottom. Then it was over the next little hill and then a straight shot to the road. I thought I knew the area real good—but I didn't. There was a gulch about twenty feet from one side to the other side. When I saw the gulch, I didn't have time to change direction, so I had to jump at a angle. That made it even longer. Kids, I gave it my all and jumped as hard as I could. I landed with one foot up on the bank and the other foot on solid ground, stumbling a little, but back in stride. Looking over my shoulder and at the same time hearing a loud grunt, I saw the sheriff going down into the gulch. Kids, I knew then I was not going to be caught, and that's when I learned how to run."

Grandpa went on with the story. He said he went to town right away so that people would see him as though he had been in town all day. Grandpa was sitting in the pool hall. He looked up and saw the sheriff coming in. Everyone started asking questions about the sheriff being outrun. The story had gotten around fast because he had never been outrun before. The sheriff admitted, "Yes, I was outrun. I don't know who the bowlegged S.O.B. was; but if I ever see him, I'll know him."

There were more questions for the sheriff. They said, "You went down in the ditch, and the man cleared it. What happened?" The sheriff said the man was wearing an overcoat with long tails, and that's what helped him jump the ditch because the tails of that coat were sticking straight out—"Hell yes, they were; a man could have shot a game of marbles on the coattails because they were so flat." After that the sheriff changed his way of doing things. I've heard the grown-ups talking about it from time to time. They said a young boy was the lookout for the moonshiners and had seen the sheriff and the revenuers coming in; he was running down the road to warn the moonshiners. From up on the top of the ridge, the sheriff took aim and fired his rifle. The sheriff's bullet hit its target, and the young boy lay down dead in the old logging road.

Two or three months went by, and Mom was saving up money for the move. Mom was also getting everything repaired, like mending the worn-out blue jeans and sewing everything up. Mom needed a pair of scissors to help with the mending. She sent my older brother and me down the road about a half mile to our neighbor's house to borrow a pair of scissors. The neighbor was real pretty and friendly. Her name was Maxine, and she liked kids. She always gave us something to drink and sometimes food. We got the scissors and started back. The neighbor's dog was following along beside us. The dog's head was bobbing up and down. My brother to this day says it was me not he that did it. My brother was opening and closing the scissors at the ear of the dog as it was bobbing up and down as he was walking. Then it happened: a big hunk of the ear fell off.

The dog was yelping and hollering, and we were trying to quiet the dog down by petting him. That was our mistake because the dog did not go to his own home. The dog went to our house and bled all over the front porch. He put his ear on the floor and slid it all over the porch, leaving a trail of blood everywhere. Mom came out to see what was happening and got cold water to wash the dog's ear. Yes, those switches that were left over were hanging up high on the porch where Grandpa had put them. Mom put those switches to use. After we had cried and then gathered ourselves, Mom said for us to go get a bucket of water, the mop, and the broom and start cleaning the porch up. While she watched us work, she was comforting the dog. When the porch was clean, we all went to the neighbor's house and Mom made us apologize. Through our tears, we finally got our apology out, explaining that we loved dogs but we moved so much that Mom and Dad would not let us have one.

Mom finally saved up the money for the move. So we moved back to our old hometown, Tullahoma, Tennessee.

Chapter 3

Babysitter Negro Clair

Coming back from Georgia, Mom found an old house outside of town on Highway 41-A. On the right side of the road going out of town toward Winchester was black town. The businesses on the main drag were white, but the blacks would go to the back door to get service. Any houses down any street from the main drag belonged to black people.

We had our little red wagon and would pull it around and play. We made our first set of stilts and walked around high up in the air. My brother learned way before I did, but I kept trying and finally got the hang of it. A black boy came up to the house one day, and we got to playing with him and became friends. We had seen black people from a distance but had not met any.

Mom wanted to go to work to help out while Dad was in the military. I really think the work was to keep her mind off Dad until his return. Somehow she got a job at Genesco Shoe Factory. Then she had to find a babysitter, and that's where our black friend came in; he told his friends about it, and here came Negro Clair. She came up and introduced herself to my mom. They talked and went in the house and did some more talking. Mom showed

Negro Clair where everything was—all the cooking stuff and food. Once Mom had a babysitter, off to work she went to make shoes for the military. Genesco had the government contract to make shoes for the army.

The days ahead of me were just to play and eat, sleep, and play some more. One day while we were eating, we boys asked Negro Clair why she did not eat anything. She said she was not supposed to eat our food, nor was she supposed to eat at the table with white folks. We all wondered why, but she got quiet and would not talk about it anymore. We boys asked Mom if it was all right if she ate and sat at the table with us. The answer was, "Yes, and you can eat or drink what you want to." After that, Negro Clair taught our younger brother how to drink coffee.

We all went to black town one day. Negro Clair had to go to town for something, and she dropped us off at her house for her daughters to watch over us while she was gone. The daughters' names were Boots and Marie, and we liked them right off. A big black boy came up the street and was getting on us asking, "What are you doing here?" We were just playing in the yard when it happened. Boots came out and told the boy to shut up, get out, and get his butt down the street before she kicked his ass. She went on to say, "We are taking care of these kids; and if you touch any one of them, I'll stomp your butt, you hear me?"

We could go anywhere we wanted to after that. Boots and Marie were pulling the wagon with our younger brother in it, and my older brother and I were walking alongside. They stopped to talk to a man about his hogs; he was feeding them acorns. We asked if we could feed them, and he said yes.

"Where did you get the acorns?" I asked.

"I got the acorns from under the trees," he said. He pointed up the street.

"Can we go get acorns and feed the pigs?"

The black man gave us two big buckets, and off we went. Putting our younger brother on the ground, we loaded the buckets in the red wagon. We picked both buckets full of the acorns and returned to the black man's pigpen. He came out, and we threw some acorns in the pen where the hogs could eat them. He said that he had fed them enough for that day, but if we came back the next day, we could feed them again. He then gave us a nickel each. We picked the trees clean of acorns the next day and got more money.

Chapter 4

We Own a House

Mom came in one day and said we were going to move to the other side of town since my older brother had to go to school. We did not want to move. We liked Negro Clair and her family. In fact, we had grown to love them over the summer months. It was the wish of Negro Clair to be called Negro Clair. She said that she had been called this all her life and there was no reason to change it now. She stated, "This is what I want to be called." We respected her wishes.

About four or five years later, Negro Clair got in touch with my mom and said Mom's brother's wife accused her of stealing a ring and other things from her. Negro Clair was crying, and her feelings were hurt. Mom went to her brother's house and told both her brother and his wife that Negro Clair did not steal. Mom chewed them out real good. Negro Clair had been doing some housecleaning for my aunt. Mom saw my aunt wearing a ring and asked her about it. Mom found out my aunt had found the ring where she hid it. My aunt said, "I was drinking and forgot where I had put it." I never did like this aunt of mine.

We moved to the other side of town, and this time my mom bought the house. I was going to be happy about the move, but did not realize it at the time. Mom met a little women about half pint size, and they became best friends. Over the years I grew to love this frisky little woman and called her my grandma. I did not have the privilege of knowing my real grandmothers.

This is my Adopted Grand Ma, ½ pint size

The house was making my mom happy, and the ownership thing just added to it. Little did she know that she was soon going back to a farm. My younger brother which I have not mentioned, is two years younger than I am. I don't remember anything about him being little or nothing. It's like Mom pick him up one day and said this is your younger brother. Now we are a family of five. Mom knew that my father would be coming home soon and was looking forward to it. The home was neat and clean, and the check coming in sure made it easier to pay off the grocery bill, every dime that was owed. Mom thanked the owner of the store several times for being so nice and helping us. The owner was so happy about the payment in full that she gave all three of us kids some candy. It took awhile to pick out the candy for us boys.

The store owner saw what was happening and asked, "Do you want something to eat real fast, or do you want something to last awhile?" We all agreed we wanted it to last awhile. This was good, and it made the long walk home a lot easier because we had our minds on the candy. The candy was caramel, called sugar daddy or the all-day sucker.

I went with my mom to the grocery store. I remember the ration tickets we received to buy coffee, butter, sugar, and smokes and other tobacco products. My older brother would watch our younger brother and try to keep him out of trouble, because he was always trying to tear up something or get into something that would make our mom mad.

Chapter 5

Rock Creek Farm

One night late, I woke up. Mom was calling my father's name out real loud and asking, "Is that you?" Mom says she heard the footsteps of my father walking across the porch. I remember Mom saying, "I know you're out there." She went to the door and opened it—and there he was.

Having my father home after the war took some getting used to. After two years of his being gone, it was different, but happy. My father started looking for work, but there was none to be had. He heard about a small farm outside town about seven miles and went to see it. My father talked my mother into selling the only home we ever owned to buy the farm. With cash in his pocket, he bought an old used truck and started buying things for the farm. Two mules and equipment, and we were farmers for the first time. We planted corn, potatoes, a garden—more than what we would use; the overage was to be sold for income.

Then my grandpa came to live with us and help out on the farm. My father went back to work at the nursery where he had worked as a young man. This was to help out and make the extra money to pay on the farm loan, which was due once a year.

There was a log house on the farm. It had an upstairs, where we boys and Grandpa made our bedrooms. The wood-boring bee—common name bumblebee—really liked the logs for some reason. They were bothersome, always buzzing around our heads. My older brother and I knew where their hole was, and we decided to take care of these bees. Our plan was to pour hot water—boiling hot water—down their hole, and that would be the end of the bumblebees. To this day, I don't remember anyone telling us that bumblebees would sting if they were made mad. My brother told me to pour the teakettle full of hot boiling water down the hole. I did just that and stepped back so my brother could pour his hot boiling water down the hole. While my brother was pouring, we heard a humming sound coming from the logs and the logs began to vibrate. All of a sudden, a bumblebee came to the edge of the hole and started to shake the water off himself. Then another. As soon as one took off and flew into the air, here came another. We started to run for the door. As I was the closest to the door, I made it inside; but my brother did not, and one of those bumblebees hit him in the nape of the neck at the hairline. The race was on: the bee stinging, my brother screaming and running around the house. The second time around, my grandpa was on the run as well, with hat in hand slapping at the bumblebee. Finally the bumblebee fell to the ground, and Grandpa stepped on him. Grandpa put his finger to his mouth and brought it out with a bunch of snuff and spit and put it on the stings. The bumblebee had stung five or six times. It was a little bit swollen, but the snuff did the trick and my brother was all right. If anyone tells you that boring bumblebees do not sting, run away from them; they are trying to get you stung.

The farm did not pay off too good. It was too small and not set up right from the start. We did not have cows to give milk for sale, nor did we have any hogs for meat or for sale. We had chickens for eggs and for frying, and that was it. My grandpa and father were soon farming part-time, and both of them worked at the nursery full-time during the winter months. Springtime both were working on the farm putting in crops during the spring planting season. When the crops were planted, they would go back to work at the nursery.

My grandfather was a wild game man and loved to eat whatever he shot or trapped. While I was watching one fall day, Grandpa built three rabbit traps and I learned a little about how to build traps. Every morning my grandfather would leave the house and go across the farm the back way. About twenty minutes later, my dad would crank up the old truck and run the road around to where my grandpa would be if there was not anything in the traps. If there was a rabbit or two, he would come back to the house before my father could crank up and leave. The traps worked really good, and Grandpa moved them around. When things were getting a little slow at the nursery, Grandpa would check the traps on the way home. He would let my dad drop him off on the road, and he would cross the woods and check the traps.

This is my Grand PA. after working all day

One evening after working all day at the nursery, Grandpa was off to check the traps. When he got home, he asked my mom to heat up some bathwater and lay out some clean clothes. My father knew something was wrong with this picture: taking a bath and putting on clean clothes in the middle of the week was unheard of. My dad started asking questions and my grandpa started getting mad, but the truth finally came out. My grandpa wore one of those old work coats called a jumper coat; they're made out of coarse cotton, with a blanket liner for warmth in the winter. The sleeves on this coat are large, and there are no wristbands. The sleeves are big on purpose, so it goes over anything else that you might be wearing.

Grandpa said, "Well hell, I might as well tell you; you are not going to stop until you know." Grandpa said he was checking the first trap at the edge of the woods because it was closed up. He pulled open the door of the trap just a little, but could not see anything except eyes looking at him. "So I ran my hand down in the trap over the back of the rabbit because it would have to be turned around to get hold of the back legs and pull it out of the trap." Grandpa soon found out it was not a rabbit because it went up the jumper sleeve at a fast rate of speed, over the back, down through the bib overalls, and out the legs of the overalls, and then ran off in the woods. A squirrel scratching all the way through leaves a long trail of scratches.

My dad said, "That still does not tell us about the clean clothes and the bath."

Grandpa said, "Accidents happen, and one did in my britches."

"Were you jumping around and hollering, Grandpa?" I asked.

"What the hell, you know I was."

We all had a good laugh. My brothers and I were mocking Grandpa, jumping around, screaming, and acting it out over and over again. Finally, my dad said, "That's enough, boys. We don't want to overdo it."

My mom was getting bigger and bigger, and we boys could not understand what was happening to her. Finally one day she explained to us that there was going to be another baby in the family.

It had been almost five years since the last child was born into the family. My mom was happy about the new one coming and acted as though it was nothing big, just another walk to the spring on a hot day. In midsummer one of the mules got loose and out of the fence where he had been kept. Mom saw the mule get loose and went to catch him, to put him back in the fenced-in area. The green grass that he had been eating must have been really good, because he did not like it when Mom grabbed the halter and pulled. He did not want to follow her. Mom pulled some more. My older brother and I were watching from a distance because we had not learned how to handle mules or horses. The mule was mad from Mom pulling on the halter, so he started to rise up on his back legs and show his teeth at my mom. Mom released the halter, and the mule began walking toward her on his back legs, showing his teeth. Mom, being scared now, turned and ran from the mule. The mule just settled down and began eating grass again.

When my younger brother was born, Mom found marks behind his right ear while bathing the baby. Mom called all of us boys to get another opinion. We all were thinking the same thing—teeth marks. Mom and Dad talked it over, and he said, "It must have been when the mule got out and showed his teeth at you." Mom admitted that she was scared that day, and it must be some kind of birthmark. My brother was okay, though.

The doctor told my mom and dad there should be no more children due to Mom's health. "When one does not listen," he said, "these things happen all over again and again. The Lord must have been looking out for her."

My older brother and I were going to a school called Center Grove School. There were only eight grades, three rooms, and three teachers. Each teacher had three rooms to teach, except for the principal; he had two grades to teach, the seventh and the eighth grade. He would do the principal work after he had the teaching work finished. The old school did not have a lunchroom and was heated by a coal heater in each room. We had to pack a lunch daily. This lunch was biscuits and eggs, biscuits and sausage, or biscuits and jelly. The school did have a milk truck that dropped off milk, but if we did not buy the milk, we had to drink water with our lunch.

We would walk up the road about a mile and ride with the neighbors and their kids to school. They had an old truck, and all of us kids would climb up in the back of the truck and ride to school. The school bus finally started coming to the top of the hill about a quarter-mile from our farm. It was only about an eighth of a mile to the neighbors' farm, but the bus was warmer than the back of the old truck and a lot safer too.

One morning we were walking up to the neighbors to catch our ride as usual and we heard a loud explosion. I mean really loud and big. When we got to the neighbors' house, they asked us to come inside the house. The son explained what had happened. He said, "The old truck would not start and had ice in the gas line. My dad was out there and had the gas tank off the truck; he poured out all the gas and blew out the gas lines. Then my dad looked down into the gas tank and thought he saw something that looked shiny like ice. Dad did not have a flashlight, so he struck a match and that's what made the loud noise."

The neighbors had a huge barn; it would have held four of our barn. It was three times higher than our barn. The son said the gas tank just missed his dad's head and went higher than the barn roof. When the tank fell back to the ground, it had blown a hole that was big enough to put a watermelon inside of the tank. When we got home that afternoon and told the story to our dad, he told us boys not to be around the neighbor when he was doing mechanical work on the truck. Dad said anyone knows that gas will blow up if there are even a few drops left to give off fumes.

This school we were going to was a mean school. The kids were mean, and there were some kids that had failed four and five times. The bathrooms were outside and to the back of the school yard. The woods in front of the outhouses shielded the view from the schoolhouse. This is where the boys smoked and did whatever they wanted to. The bigger boys would pick up a little boy, such as I, and try to shove him down the hole in the outhouse. The boys did this to me several times, but they could not get the job done. The rules of the game the big boys played were that only one could try to do the shoving down the hole and no one could help out or the game was over. I always got them to tire out and the boy would have to release me. When we little ones were released, you should have seen us running for the schoolhouse.

The big boys made it a challenge to grab me. When the bell rang for recess, I would be out the door and running as fast as I could to the outhouse to get my business done and over with and be gone before the big boys showed up.

My brother and I were picked on every day, and we were telling our dad but he was not listening. One day when I got home, my ear was bleeding and I could not hear. I had a ringing in my ears. My brother and I said, "We are not going back to that school." We told Mom that the big girls had pulled on my ears so hard that they had started to bleed. Then one of the big girls, when I was not looking, came and slapped both of my ears at the same time. My head hurt, and the ringing in my ears did not let up for four days. These girls were fifteen and sixteen years old and still in the seventh and eighth grades.

Finally my dad had enough and went to the school with us. When we got there, the classes were already in progress. Our dad walked into the classroom and asked for the principal. The students were pointing to the principal, at a table in the back to the right of the big room. Dad told the principal what trouble we were having and said, "I want it to stop right now. If the trouble doesn't stop, I will come here and kick your tail for you."

The principal said, "There is very little I can do." He pushed back from the table that he was using for a desk. The principal was crippled, and his wheelchair was against the wall. Dad saw this and apologized to the principal, and then he told both of us boys to walk around and get in front of him. We did as he said. Dad had his hands on our shoulders. Looking straight at the other kids, Dad spoke to them. "Take a good look at my boys. I'm telling you now, if any one of you boys or girls hurts one of my boys again, I will come to your house and kick your mother's and father's butts. I had better not have to come out here again. Did I make it clear enough for you kids?" He repeated it again. Dad then looked at the principal and told him to get another teaching job, that being a principal was not for him.

The trouble stopped, and my brother and I were happy. We were going to leave this school real soon. But before our moving around stopped, we would be back to this school.

Chapter 6

Overpass Apartment

We moved again, this time back to town, because the farm was not paying off as it should be, according to my father. My dad sold everything but the house furniture and personal belongings. We had only the mules left to sell. We had eaten all the chickens up, and there were no eggs left. The chicken must be there before the egg, or there are no eggs.

Work in town could not be found. My dad signed up for the army again. Dad told my mom that the allotment money would be more now since there were four boys now. Dad said another hitch in the army would be good. And when the hitch was up, maybe he could find a good-paying job when he got out.

We moved into an upstairs apartment. The apartment was at the end of an overpass for the railroad. Would you believe that my adopted grandma was going to be our next-door neighbor? Grandma had lost her home too. Her husband was a drinking man, and he spent all his money on drinking whiskey and beer. Grandma's husband finally drank himself to death. Grandma had lost everything and moved into an apartment. Bill, Grandma's oldest son, was in the air force and put her on the allotment; he was taking care of his mom and brother.

When Bill came home on leave and needed something from the store, he would call on me for the errand. I would have to tell my mom first, and off I would go on the errand. When I got back, he would give me some money. This would make me feel big and important.

My father would come home on leave and stay about a week before going back to Fort Knox, Kentucky. One time my father brought home some boxing gloves.

Dad was going to teach us how to box and defend ourselves. He started with my older brother. "Here is how you throw a punch, and here is how you block a punch." Then came my turn, and it was fun until I got my head hurting. That was it for me. My father had been drinking beer and would not let me stop. He pushed me even harder to learn the art of boxing. My brother or my mom must have gotten his attention, because he turned his head to me and I roundhoused him as hard as I could. My dad, from reflexes, swung a punch and hit me in the head, knocking me down the stairs head over heels a couple times. At the bottom of the stairs, I could hear my dad running down the stairs, asking, "Are you all right? Is anything broken?" I said I didn't think so and got up and pulled off the gloves. I didn't have the headache anymore. My dad handed the gloves back to my brother and at the top of the stairs, started boxing again.

Mom went to the hospital and had my baby sister. A new member of the family, and Mom and Grandma were very happy and smiling from ear to ear. A girl in the family, which already had four boys. Grandma was taking care of the family while Mom was in the hospital. Somewhere Grandma learned how to make biscuit pudding, and she saved up the leftover biscuits from breakfasts. When she had plenty of them, as we watched, she crumbled the biscuits up for the pudding. She put all the ingredients in and stirred it up real good so the biscuits could soak up all the flavors. We were off to play. Grandma cooked the pudding while we were playing and called all of us boys to eat. We were thinking just of eating pudding. But she had cooked up some other stuff and said we had to eat and clean up the plates before we could have some of the pudding. Not knowing the taste of the pudding, we ate everything clean from our plates. Then the pudding came, and it was really good. That was the first time I got to know what biscuit pudding was. Mom came home from the hospital, and we could not wait to tell Mom about the biscuit pudding and ask her to learn how to make it.

Chapter 7

Ella Ransom Homes

Mom had heard about some apartments for poor people, with subsidized rent for the ones that qualified. We qualified because Dad was in the military. There was not an open apartment right then, but the wait was only three weeks. So we moved again. I had begun to hate moving. I had to help mostly with the small boxes and tearing the beds down after the mattresses were removed. We would leave friends behind and have to make new ones over and over again. Yes, I hated moving. I know that now.

We moved. Mom explained the rent would be cheaper, and that we needed three bedrooms now that there was a girl in the family.

This neighborhood was mean, and the kids would do anything. From rock throwing to stealing, cussing, fighting, or whatever. The parents were never home: the father was working or in the military, and the mother was at work. Some families had only one parent. This gave free rein for the kids to do whatever they wanted. They did not have any chores to do; and back in those days, no one had heard of allowances for the children. In summer when school was out, it was hell somewhere in the neighborhood almost every day.

We were new to the neighborhood, and this meant that we were the ones to be picked on. There were fights almost every day, and Mom gave us permission to protect ourselves any way we could.

This is what would happen. My brother led the way; since he knew how to box, the rest of the kids were no match for him. We kicked butts whenever we were picked on. I learned how to throw rocks like a national champion. I figured out how to choose the perfect rocks and had two pockets full at all times. Mom would make me empty my pockets before I came into the apartment. I had to get a bag and put them in the bag because the kids would steal my handpicked rocks because they were too lazy to pick out their own. We fought almost daily.

One day we had thirty or more kids in front of the house at one time shouting and saying bad names. It just so happened that my father was home on leave and wanted to know what was going on. Mom explained the problem. My father said to my older brother and me, "Get sticks or whatever you need, and go run them off." I went and got a broom that was a throwaway broom and sawed off the handle so it would be short enough for me to handle. My brother chose his fists and said, "That's all I will need." Out the door we went. My father said, "Whip their butts, or I will whip yours."

We did just that. While they were shouting and running their mouths, we walked right up to them. The one with the loudest mouth was hit square in it by my brother. We were knocking heads one after the other. Then a big girl, I would say about seventeen, stepped out to confront my brother by kicking at his head. My brother sidestepped, ducked under and caught her leg, and lifted it up higher than it was supposed to go. Her head hit the hard ground, knocking her out. When this happened, kids flew in all directions. We continued to run after them a little ways. The playground was empty except for my brother and me.

We looked at each other, and we both smiled as if to say, "You think our dad will be proud of us?" He was, and he said, "That's the way to defend yourselves."

There were three fights that week. The kids kept getting bigger and bigger and older each time. I was in a fight with my broomstick in hand and put a couple of knots on their heads. Then this big, big boy said some nasty trash talk to me for doing the head knocking. I, getting brave, grabbed the tarp that he was working on, jerked it loose, and pulled it as I ran up the street. The big, big boy was after me, so I dropped the tarp and ran as fast as I could. Being small, I just made the back door of the apartment. My father was sitting at the table eating when I came through. My father saw the big hand reaching after me just scratching lightly on the back of my shirt and grabbed the wrist. By that time the big, big boy was in the house. My father popped his nose and gave him a good shaking and told him if he ever touched one of us boys that he would kick his butt. Then my brother got into it with another big, big, I mean big boy, and my brother bloodied his nose.

The police came out to the apartment on each occasion. My father all three times explained that every time one of us kids was outside of the house, we were jumped on. "The police should be talking to the parents and the other children," he stated. The police told my father the other families had been here longer than we had. We found out later that the boy that came in the house was nineteen years old. The police did nothing about it.

One day late in the summer, Mom was getting her hair done just down the street about four doors. Mom would do ironing and housecleaning for the hairdresser, now called a beautician, in exchange for her hair being done. Mom did the work weekly and when she did not have to have her hair done, she would keep the money.

I was sitting on the back steps with a couple of friends and my younger brothers when a girl about sixteen years of age started walking up and down in front of us. She was twisting her hips and talking trash talk. Her girlfriends were around the corner peeping out from time to time and asking her to do more things. Then she started calling our family names, and my younger brother confronted her. The girl, being much bigger, stronger, and older, just pushed my brother to the ground. The girl and I had an exchange of words, which just spurred her to worse name calling. I always had two pockets of rocks, and I pulled out a handful and told her to leave. She would not, and so I threw a couple of warning shots. I again asked her to shut up and leave, and she would not. I threw another rock to make her stop talking trash and leave. The rock hit the back of her head, and she started stumbling and walking toward the corner of the house where her friends were. She fell to the ground unconscious. This scared me to no end. I didn't want to kill her; I just wanted her to shut up and quit calling my family names.

I ran down the street to the beauty shop where my mom was getting her hair done; she was under the hairdryer. I slid under the chair, and Mom wanted to know what was wrong. I told her that I had thrown a rock and hit this girl and she might be dead because she fell to the ground and was not moving. We came out of the beauty shop on the run. When we got there, a group of people had gathered to see what had happened. The girl went to the doctor, and it took fourteen stitches to sew her head up. We went to the house where the girl lived, and no one was at home. Mom left a note saying that we would be back that afternoon. We did go back, and my mom apologized and asked if the girl was okay. The girl's father wanted for us to pay the bill. Mom refused and told them that it was the girl's fault for cussing and calling our family names out in front of our house and that she should have been at home. We left, feeling bad for the girl.

When we went back to school in the fall, almost all of these fights stopped. During the winter, I got sick with pneumonia, which I had before. We went to the doctor and I got a shot of penicillin;

I was on my way to healing. Then I caught it again. The doctor called it double pneumonia this time, and I felt cold all the time. All the time I would wear my coat, which was a mackinaw coat. The kids in the neighborhood made fun of me for wearing the coat. I finally stopped wearing the coat the end of June or the first week of July.

One night late, my mother woke up and heard noises. She called to my brothers and me, asking what the noises were. We told her it was not us, that we were not making the noise. There were so many in the bed that we had not noticed one was missing. It was my younger brother. We all got up and started looking for him. Mom said she thought she had heard the back door open. We all went to the door. What did we see? My brother was walking around in a circle, humming while rubbing his belly, just as naked as a jaybird. There was a streetlight, and anyone looking would not have a problem seeing what was going on. I don't think my brother was humming a country song, because I did not recognize it. The next day Mom took him to the doctor, and the doctor gave her some medicine in a great big old bottle. I never did find out what was wrong. When we asked Mom, she said the doctor said he would grow out of it and be okay. He did, and he is sixty-eight years old this year.

The last time the police came out when my father was home, they asked my dad, "I thought you were going to move."

My dad answered, "Why should we move? My boys have whipped everyone in the neighborhood."

The police drove off. They were shaking their heads and talking, laughing as they left. After that, everything was calm; and the other kids in the neighborhood became friends or just paid us no never-mind. It never bothered us a bit; in fact, the neighborhood was quite livable now.

Spring came, and I was glad and happy, tired of all the colds and being sick all the time. Spring meant warm weather and feeling good again.

In May we had a new member added to the family. It was another baby girl. This would be my mom's last child. The doctors repeated their admonition for her not to have any more children.

Chapter 8

Robinson's Farm

My father was home from the military. There was no work again, and so off we went to another farm. This time it was out of the county. It was in Bedford County at a spot called Deason, Tennessee. It was known as Robinson's Farm, and horses were running everywhere, wild as wild could get. I don't know how my father found these places. When asked, he would just say, "I did," and let it go at that. We had plenty of time to get settled in and get firewood for the winter, what we thought would be enough. But as usual, we were not right. Grandpa had come to live with us again. His wife, my grandmother, died when she was forty-two years of age. I think Grandpa was lonesome and needed company. He had been around children all his life, because he had six children.

The winter started early that year. We were wearing our coats already in the fall, and we didn't think summer was completely over. We only had about two and a half miles to go to school. This was an old school, with only three rooms to it. There was the lunch kitchen, where they cooked the meals and the meals were served; you went back to your desk to eat the lunch. There was another room off to one side, but it was closed off; it had leaks in the roof and a window or two broken out, so the old classroom was not used. The big classroom had a stage at the end, and the rest of the room was set up for all eight grades. A large stove sat up front between the stage and the classroom for winter heat. In the winter months, all the kids had to wear their coats to stay warm. Every morning all of us boys that were old enough went to school. Our favorite song on the radio, WSM at that time, was "The Tennessee Stud," by Tennessee Ernie Ford. When the song was finished, out the door we went running and singing the song all the way to the schoolhouse.

The wood starting running short about the end of January. This meant cutting up more wood. It was a hard winter. I could hear the grown-ups talk about it, saying it was the coldest in several years. That meant burning more wood to keep warm.

On a Friday night, the big snow came, and we were trying to dig out. We had to open up the paths to the woodpile and the spring where we got the drinking and cooking water. The outhouse path had to be opened up also, and the chicken house so the chickens could be fed. Grandpa had gotten up to make the fire burn high to make more heat for the house and to get the fire going in the kitchen stove for hot coffee and breakfast. The coffee was for the grown-ups. Grandpa went out of the house and came back in shortly. He was telling my dad that there was so much snow out there that it was knee-high to a jackass. It was, too.

The next morning we all—my dad, Grandpa, my older brother, and myself—dressed as warmly as we could and headed off to the woods to cut wood. My brother and I were introduced to the cross saw. My dad and Grandpa would get the trees on the ground and trim them up. We would measure out blocks going up the tree toward the little end. My brother and I would saw block after block until exhausted; then we would take a break time to warm up. My father had built a fire for warming up, and I liked it because my hands had began to hurt from the cold. We worked the rest of the day and Sunday. We still had not cut enough wood to last the winter.

With school called off due to the snow—which did not mean anything to our father because he had woodcutting on his mind—it was back to the woods. We cut wood for the next four days. My father was busting the blocks, and he and Grandpa together were cutting down the trees. Then Grandpa would do the trimming up. Everyone had a job to do. My father said that he and Grandpa would haul the wood up later to the house.

My hands had chapped and cracked open from the cold and from being in the snow. I had begun to cry a little bit from the pain, taking frequent breaks to warm up my cold hurting hands. I don't cry very easily, but I was hurting.

My grandpa asked me if I wanted to cure my chapped hands. I said yes, of course, and asked how to do it. My grandpa told me to go over behind the trees, pull down my britches, tinkle on my hands, and wash my hand in the tinkle. I looked at my dad to get approval and asked if it was true that it would cure my chapped hands. He said, "If Gramps says so, then it's true." With some doubt, I proceeded over behind the trees and pulled down my britches, which dropped around my ankles. I needed relief from the cold chapped hands that were open and bleeding now from the cold. I was willing to try anything at this point. So I started tinkling and washing my hands in the warm tinkling, which felt so good. Then I began hollering and screaming, jumping, hollering, screaming, and crying. My britches wrapped around my feet, and I fell in the snow. I got right back up and pulled my britches up. I looked over at my dad and my grandpa, and both were laughing and clapping their hands. My brother was laughing, too, but not as hard as the other two were. Every time for the rest of the day that I looked over at them, they would be grinning from ear to ear, showing their shiny teeth like a mule's butt with teeth in it.

It hurt and was painful, but it did the trick. My hands started to heal up real good. I had chapped hands from time to time, but this did something to cure the chapping. Fatback bacon grease or anything else would not work, but this worked. One problem solved out of so many. So this is what is meant when you hear someone say, "Piss on it." If it's a cure, then it's great.

My next-younger brother caught the measles, and Mom told me to watch him and not let him out of the house, that the cold snow would drive the measles in and he would die from it. I got busy doing something, and I heard the front door open up and out the door my brother went, naked and running and laughing. Out the door I went to fetch him, grabbing him and pulling him back in the house. Yeah, I got a whipping and a chewing out. Everyone was scared that my brother was going to die. He did not die, though, and yes, he is the same brother that was walking around naked about a year earlier.

Spring finally came, and the planting season was to get underway. My father and Grandpa were planning where to plant what. We put in cotton, corn, and a big garden. We had two horses that would work, and that they did. My father talked to the owner about the rest of the horses and mules. The owner said that the old mule, he thought, had been worked a long time ago. This would work out real good if the mule would work. My father caught the old mule after we kids ran them all up to the barn. The bridle and harness were put on, and then we went off to test it out. The mule was a little bit nervous but settled down nicely and was a good working mule.

The mule had one gait when pulling the plow or any other equipment. The speed was too fast for my dad to keep up; he had to almost run or jog. He tried to slow her down, but she would not slow. He put all his weight on the plow and sank it deep in the ground. This did not work either. Being worn out, Dad unhooked the mule and put her in the barn and fed her. The next Saturday, my brother was to help, because my father had a plan. Dad said, "We will take turns. I will go first, and then you can go. This way we will wear her down, and she will be all right." After about two hours of this over and over again, both my father and brother were worn out. Then the old mule had all she could take, and off she went on the run pulling the plow. The plow hooked a fence post and jerked the fence out of the ground because the fence was old and rotting. The mule ran all the way to the barn.

Later in the summer, they would try again. The corn was up about six feet high and looking good. We were chopping cotton and hoeing out the grass. My father asked for my brother to come with him to help. My father put my brother on the bridle and said, "Lead her along the row and slow her down while I plow." This was called the double shovel, and it tore up about three rows just in places. The old mule went to sling her head and shook my brother loose, and off she went, but not far. They started again, and this time it worked. Dad was in good shape, having been in the army for two terms. He said, "I can run pretty good, but not all day like this b---- can."

The owner came out often to check on the farm and look at the crops. This is when I got my nickname Cotton Top. The owner said, "Son, your hair is as white as cotton." The name stuck. Some of my friends still refer to me as old man Cotton Top. I will explain later how they knew my nickname.

My dad and the owner of the place had a deal about the farm on splitting the crops. The owner also had a deal about feeding his hogs and the animals on a day-to-day basis. We kids all pitched in and fed the hogs and did the chores. One day on the weekend, the owner was talking to all of us boys about his hogs; and we pointed out that one of the little pigs had a funny-looking leg. We pointed it out with our little fingers, all at the same time. He went and checked it out and agreed that it was a deformed leg. We kids told him that we had been looking out for him, not letting the other pigs push him out where he could not get anything to eat. The owner said, "You boys want a pig?" Yes, everyone said at the same time. My older brother said we would have to check with our dad before we could have him.

Dad was asked, and he said we didn't have the feed to feed the pig. The owner said, "You boys have been doing a good job. Each day after feeding, take what you need to feed the pig." We all jumped up and down. You talk about being happy—we were. Dad said, "You have got to build a pen before you can get the pig." Build a pen we did. My older brother and I started rounding up what we needed to build the pen. Our younger brother was not much help, and we told him he could go to the house and help Mom. Truth was, he was getting in the way and slowing us down on our building. We worked the rest of the afternoon. After breakfast on Sunday morning, we were at it again. Monday and Tuesday afternoon after school, we finished up and had time to bring him back to the pen and turn him loose. We admired the pig. We thought he was the greatest pig in the world; and to us boys, who never owned anything in our lives, he was.

We fed him every day, and he began to grow. We were proud. We kids were talking about what to name our pig. Several names were suggested. Our oldest brother came up with pork chop, and so the pig became known as Pork Chop.

Midsummer came, and was it hot. There would be days that no wind or air was stirring around, and this made it hotter. We got our drinking, cooking, and bath water from the spring. The days we were in the fields, it was cooler on us than at the house. The way the house set, the little hill behind it made the air flow up and over the house. On Saturdays and Sundays, we would be in the woods or by the pond. One Sunday early morning, we boys were outside the house playing just after breakfast. We heard a noise like a car and looked up; it was my mom's brother and his wife and family. Yes, this is the aunt that told the lie to the babysitter. The car stopped at the yard fence, and they were getting out of the car. They were wiping the sweat off their brows and panting from the heat. My aunt was saying, "I think I can drink a gallon of water."

My Family at one of the old Farms. My Head is behind my younger Brother's head and I guess my oldest Brother was taking Picture. No one in family remembers. We did not have or own a camera.

My dad said, "Boys, show her where to get a drink of water."

I said okay. I took her over to the well and told her I would draw up a bucket of water that would be real cold. I filled the bucket and drew it up. My aunt grabbed the dipper, which hung on the well post. My aunt got a dipper full and started drinking the water real fast; she drank the whole dipper full of water. She was reaching to fill the dipper up again, and the taste and smell got in her mind. She dropped the dipper on the ground and stepped over about three steps and started vomiting, holding her stomach. I think breakfast and the water both came up. I was laughing, and everyone started laughing with me. I told my aunt that it was sulfur water. She said, "It smells like rotten eggs." Then my aunt said, "You little devil, you did this on purpose, didn't you?" I had to admit to it and I said yes, and we all starting laughing again. My aunt was mad that the joke was on her.

My mom started to give orders. Mom said, "You boys, catch three of those biggest chickens." We already knew not to catch the laying hens. We were holding the chickens, and Dad came out and started wringing the heads off the chickens. Dad went back in the house, because he knew that my uncle would have a bottle of whiskey with him. My aunt came over to where we were plucking the chickens. My aunt asked us boys, "Did you know that a rooster can break wind?"

Laughing, we said, "No, they can't."

She said, "Yes, they can. Let me have the chicken." She got the chicken with a hand on each side and made a circle with the chicken around and around. On the way around, the chicken made a sound of breaking wind. All of us boys jumped back and started laughing about the chicken that broke wind.

The dinner was good, and we all ate our fill of the chicken and gravy. The corn, fried okra, taters, and cathead biscuits were delicious.

There was an old sorghum mill up the road toward the barn. We asked Dad what it was, and he explained that it presses out the sweet juice from the cane and pointed to the field next to the corn. I had thought it was all corn. Dad went on to tell us when the cane got ripe, we would cut it and run it through the mill and get the juice. Then we would have to build a fire and cook the sorghum until done and thick to hold on a biscuit. It was very important not to get it too hot and let it burn and stick to the bottom of the cooking pan. If this happened, it would not be good to eat.

When it came time, we all including my mom made the sorghum. It was good every morning on the big cathead biscuits. Then she made sorghum bread, and it turned out to be a treat.

The cotton had begun to open up, and we were told what that meant. Picking time was not far off. The schools back in those days closed up for three weeks in some counties and two in other counties. We picked and plucked cotton until our hands got sore, and we soaked them in saltwater every night to get the soreness out so we could pick the next day. We did the same thing when the corn was ready and gathered all the garden. Mom canned up everything she could from the garden as the vegetables came in. We were ready for the winter.

Well, not hardly ready. I had forgotten about Pork Chop, our prize hog. Pork Chop's weight was at about three hundred pounds. My younger brother had been riding him like a horse until my mom made him stop. Mom told him that riding would take off all the fat. The weather had turned cold, and Grandpa had been helping the neighbors kill their hogs. The day we knew was coming finally arrived, and my father said it was hog-killing time. We could not watch; it was sad for us to lose our prize hog. Dad explained that when we started eating the pork sausages and all the good things from the hog, we would forget all about Pork Chop. We did. My brother ate so many that he got sick and was visiting the outhouse all through the night. The whole family had a laugh about it.

And then there was the polecat, or skunk, which I was not familiar with. This incident happened early that year, just after spring broke real good. I knew that the skunk was black and white and smelled bad. I did not know that he would spray it out like a water gun. My father loved chicken meat and eggs. He bought all of the laying hens and one old rooster to take care of the hens. He also bought two dozen little chicks, just babies, and we had them in a coop so they would get a little bigger before we released them to make it on their own. One morning coming back from the barn, I saw a skunk coming out of the yard, carrying one of our baby chicks in its mouth. I ran toward them looking for a stick or something to knock the chick loose and free him from the skunk. I found a piece of a two-by-four lying by the gate, which we had been using to prop the gate open. I grabbed the two-by-four and ran toward them; they were out in the field by then. I realized where the skunk was headed. It was a sinkhole out in the field of corn. I ran around and got in front of the skunk. The skunk turned his back to me, and I ran around again to his front; this happened again. I was trying to get to the front to knock the baby chick loose; the chick was still alive, and I wanted to save it from the skunk.

I was still holding the two-by-four. Just as the skunk turned back around toward me, I brought it down, trying to hit the skunk in the back to make it release the baby chick. I did not judge the length of the two-by-four right. I hit the skunk in the head. The head went to the ground. This meant the butt was in the air. Then here came the spray, like it was aimed directly at me. The spray hit me right in the eyes. I was on fire. Stumbling around I was slowly finding my way to the house. Every time I opened my eyes to see where I was going, the burning was so bad I had to close my eyes again. My eyes had tears coming out of them, but I was not crying. I started calling for my mom. The third time I called she heard and came running.

Mom realized what had happened and ran and got the bucket of water and splashed it in my face. This did not work too well. Mom thought of the spring and led me toward it. Mom told me to lie on the ground and splash the water in my face. I did, but it was still burning. I thought about ducking my head down in the water and did. This was what I called relief. I had to come up for air, and I soon learned to keep my eyes closed. When I came up for air with my eyes open, my eyes would be on fire again. I kept ducking my head and opening my eyes while underwater, holding my breath. I did this for about one and a half hours. It finally felt better and I got up, but not for long. Back to lying down again and ducking, opening and closing my eyes to wash them out. This went on for about thirty more minutes. Finally I got up and got my breath back. I started for the house, but Mom called out and said, "Pull off your clothes and let them lay in the yard. Go and wash with this soap, and then you can come in the house. Here are some more clothes."

I went and checked on the baby chick after I told Mom what I was trying to do. The chick was dead, and so was the skunk. My father said that the skunks had a den down in the sinkhole and had young babies. The skunks were teaching the young how to kill and eat and how to get the smell in their minds for hunting food.

Those were the newest bib overalls that I had. Mom tried to save them by washing them several times and letting them hang on the line in the sunshine. Every time Mom would iron, she would try to iron the bib overalls, but the stink just kept coming out and I finally had to throw them away.

I found out years later that if I had washed my face and clothes in tomato juice, every bit of the smell would have come out—and it would have stopped the burning eyes.

There was a little church in Deason, the Church of God. Mom wanted us to go with her to church. Mom went two or three times to get us three oldest boys started, so we started going to church that summer after school was out. After Mom turned us loose, we went to church only a month of Sundays, that means four.

We loved the little church, though we did not understand what the preacher was talking about. It was all new to us, and we watched and noticed everything. The people would glance at us from time to time and to one another and roll their eyes. We knew what this meant; we were poor, not stupid. We knew that we were poor, dressed poor, looked poor, had no money poor, and acted poor, so we did not need anyone telling us about it. Just about the time we were catching on and learning about the Bible, we felt unwelcome and quit going to the little church. Sometimes I think Mom and Dad wanted us three oldest boys out of the house, so they could let the three youngest kids take a nap and they could play house again.

My wife and I drove through the little town on our way to my twenty-five-year class reunion, going to my hometown. The little church was gone. The schoolhouse was still there. It's a community center and a historical landmark for the little town.

Christmas came, and we had lots to eat. Dad got some oranges, apples, nuts, and candy, and Mom put up a little tree. Mom showed us how to sew popcorn to put it on a string. Mom put it on the tree for decoration. Mom said this was the first Christmas that the whole family was there after completion. We did not have any presents or anything, but we had treats of fruits and candy. It was enough to please us kids because we did not know any better or know of any other way of having Christmas.

My father came home from somewhere. After he came in the house, right out of the blue, he said, "We've got to move around the first of March. I have made a deal with the brother of the owner to take over his big farm. I've looked at it. It's a bigger farm. He has two farm tractors and milk cows. We milk the cows, and every two weeks we split the milk money. It's going to be better for all of us."

I asked about the wood that we had just cut. "Dad, we're not going to leave the wood, are we? That's the wood that we cut in the coldest part of the winter."

My dad said, "We will cut some more; it's too much trouble to haul."

In the process of moving, Dad borrowed a big truck from the owner for moving; it would do just fine for moving the wood. I asked the owner of the place if we could take the wood with us. He said, "Sure—if you load it up."

My dad started chewing me out for asking.

The owner said, "I don't blame him. If I had cut the wood, I would want it too."

My dad got onto me before at the potato digging. Big, I mean real big, potatoes were falling out of the dirt. My eyes could not believe it. We had put a little piece of a potato in the dirt, and all these came out. I was saying, "Gaa–lee, look at this one."

My dad got onto me for saying "Gaa–lee," which I did not think was bad. He said, "Watch your mouth, big boy."

The owner said, "He has not said anything wrong or bad. I'm surprised, too; these are the biggest potatoes ever. I did not think this ground would be rich enough to grow crops this good." The owner had stuck up for me twice now, and it made me feel good.

Chapter 9

Burton's Farm

We finally got the move made. It was the first time I had seen the large house; I couldn't believe we were going to live there. It was a huge house. There was a front porch. The house had two stories and looked like it had rooms everywhere. Going through the front door, a large room to the left was Dad and Mom's chosen room. The room to the right was going to be left empty. Going down a short hall, another door led to another bedroom, which was going to be Grandpa's room. Over to the left of the room was a door to a staircase; upstairs were two rooms. Mom said we boys would be sleeping in these two rooms. In the bedroom directly below, on the other side was another door, which led into the giant room where the fireplace was. It was the largest room in any house that I had ever been in. Straight through from the door we came through was another door, to the kitchen. It was a large kitchen, with dining room added in. There was plenty of room for all of us. Off to the right was a pantry with a lot of shelves and plenty of room for storing canned goods and food. Going out the back door in the room where the fireplace was led to a huge L-shaped back porch with steps at both ends.

The steps at the end of the house, out from the kitchen, led to the chicken coops and the outhouse. In between the house and the chicken coops and the yard fence was the biggest tree in a yard that I had ever seen. Little did I know that it would be bigger yet when the leaves got on it. Down the porch at the other end led toward the barns and the garage with a storage loft in it. The woodpile was to the left and closest to the house, which was a good thing. When carrying wood, every step saved helps. The barn and milk barn were all built together, the milk barn on the right as you walked to the barn. It was big. It was going to take time to get the full concept of this huge barn. On the way back to the house, I noticed the woodpile was about empty; I was glad I had asked about the wood. The wood would be unloaded the next day and the truck returned.

The room chosen for us boys was going to be great, but at that time we did not know it. We carried everything up the stairs and set our room up.

The next morning, four thirty was early for us to get up. It took awhile to get our eyes open and set off to the barn. Today we boys would learn how to milk a cow. My older brother caught on real fast how to milk; now all he had to do was build up the speed of the milking. It was harder for me because my hands were too small for the big tits. Then my dad got an idea about three days later to put me on the jersey cows, which had smaller tits. It all worked out.

After taking the milk to the house, my brother and I went to wash up for breakfast. We had to eat and get ready for school, and we had to hurry every morning and run out to catch the school bus. This was the first school bus we ever rode that came right to the front door of the house. We started to school at Unionville and finished out the year.

Then summer came, and school was out. We were glad. It was hard to come in from school and just get a snack of corn bread and a glass of milk. We had to get our homework done right then and get out and carry wood up onto the porch and get the wood for the kitchen stove. Then it was off to the barn to milk four or five cows. It would be dark when we came in during the winter months. We would wash up and get ready for supper. Then we would hang out for a little while and then it was off to bed, to sleep as fast as one could, because four thirty came early in the morning.

Dad and Grandpa put the crops in. About halfway through planting season, the Smith brothers, who had some kind of deal with Mr. Burton, came over to start their planting. They had an old man working with them, and his name was Robert. The old man was bent over in the shoulders as though he was going forward at all times. He had the heel built up on his left shoe about three and a half inches. This was why he continually leaned forward. He was cutting a tree down and the tree fell across his leg, breaking it in five places. He was a worker; just give him a job to do without much walking in it, and the work was done. He would become our adopted uncle, but at this time, neither we nor he knew that this was going to happen.

Late in the spring planting season, the Smith brothers were planting corn in a field that you could see from the house. They had the corn planter on the back of a Massey Fergerson Ford. I was riding the corn planter and watching the fertilizer hopper and was to tell them when one or the other ran almost out, so adjustments could be made so they would run out at the same time. This way both could be filled up at the same time, and all the corn would get a little fertilizer and grow the same.

I did not know how the hopper was built. I started dipping the fertilizer with my hand and putting the fertilizer in the other hopper. I finally had it even and waved to the Smith boy, who was about twenty-one, letting him know to keep going to the end of the row for the adjustments and to fill up with fertilizer. Then I would not leave well enough alone. I put my hand deep in the hopper again, and my finger got caught in the two cogs that were turning. They mashed off the end of my big middle finger. Blood was everywhere, and I was screaming bloody murder as loud as I could holler.

As soon as I could get off the Ford, I took off running to the house. I looked up through my tears and saw my dad coming down the lane on the run. He asked if the Smith boy had done it, and I said no. We went to the house, washed it in cold water, and wrapped it up in a wet towel. By that time the Smith boy had showed up to find out what happened. As soon as he saw it, he told me to get in the car. "I'm carrying you to the doctor." Off we went. The old doc eased the pain and sewed up the end of my finger. By the time I got back home, the pain had returned. The only painkiller back then was to take two aspirin and grit your teeth until the pain stopped. I slept that night with my arm sticking up in the air. Every time my heart beat, I could feel it in my finger if I had it laying down.

Mom said my dad had jumped the fence out back, which was a cow fence of four foot, topped by two strings of barbed wire. This made the fence about five and one half feet high. Mom said Dad was running and put one hand on the fence post and over he went.

My grandpa did not like milking the cows. Grandpa also did not take a shine to Robert. Somehow they just did not like one another. Grandpa decided to go back to live with one of his sons. My dad made a deal with Robert to stay with us and help with the milking and the farmwork. He moved into the house across the hall to the right of Mom and Dad's room, where no one had been staying. This old man was fascinating, with his tales of everything he talked about. Robert said that he had walked all the way to Texas and walked back after living out there for three years. Grandpa could not outdo him when it came to telling tales. We kids adopted the old man and started calling him Uncle Robert, and he became part of the family.

Summer came. Grandpa must have told his son, our uncle, my Mom's brother, that we had a good setup and were doing good.

The crops had been gathered and the cotton sold, and we were getting ready for winter. We were putting up firewood for the winter. This farm made it a lot easier to get the firewood. We could cut the wood in the woods and haul it to the house on the farm wagon pulled by the tractor; or we could cut the trees down and trim them up and drag them to the woodpile to be cut up later. We did it both ways. The fires in the fireplace felt good coming in from the barn after milking. The room that we boys slept in was warm, because the fireplace chimney ran up through the house. This was the warmest room that we had while living on the farms. We could get out of bed and get dressed without the chill bumps.

Christmas was near when one weekend here came my uncle, my Mom's brother, and his family. It was his second wife and she had kids of her own, and two of her sisters lived with them. Their mom had died, and the oldest sister was trying to give them a home.

They stayed two nights with us, and everyone had a good time. The grown-ups played a card game called Rook. The kids played checkers and games, but mostly talked and watched the grown-ups from a distance. Mom put on some good home-cooked meals, and everyone was full when they left the table. When the time came to leave, the oldest sister of my uncle's wife wanted to stay two weeks with us. Mom and Dad said okay, but she would have to do some chores for my mom. All agreed. Then my uncle and his family were on their way home.

Mom had taken all the girls out to the outhouse to show it to them when they first got there for the visit. After three or four nights had gone by, the girl got up in the morning and went out to the outhouse. Early every morning Uncle Robert would get up and clean the fireplace of the ashes and put them in a five-gallon metal bucket and set them on the back porch to cool off because some of the coals were still alive with the fire. After they cooled down, he would return and dump them. In the meantime, he would put on fresh wood and build the fire up really big to warm the house.

The girl must have seen the bucket sitting there and changed her mind about going to the outhouse. So she tinkled in the bucket. She must have been wanting to go bad and let it all come out at once. Steam came up from the hot ashes. When the steam burned the girl all over her tinkling spot, she screamed like a stuck pig. Mom ran out on the back porch and grabbed her by the arm to see what had happened. Her drawers were down around her ankles. She pulled them up with one hand and followed my mom into the kitchen.

Mom came out and told us what had happened, which we already knew. Mom said she had put some butter on the burn and the girl would be fine in a couple of days. All of us boys had fun making jokes about the incident. Someone said if she had been wearing eyeglasses, they would have steamed up and she would have jumped off the back porch. Although we all had fun about it, we did feel sorry for her and did not make any jokes where she could hear them.

We stayed on this farm a little over two years, and there was something going on all the time. I'll try to tell one or two of the stories. There was a little jersey cow who got down when she had a baby calf; then she could not get back up. My older brother and I pulled her over by the hind legs to a place between two trees and tied up a sling to hold up the cow. We could not do it by ourselves, and we got Uncle Robert and Dad to help us. We two brothers carried food and water to her every day and tried to get her to move her legs, but she would not make the effort. The jersey cow kept going down, and we lost her. The good thing was that Uncle Robert got one of the other cows to nurse the calf, and it did okay.

Uncle Robert had killed a chicken snake out at the barn and brought it to the woodpile. He told my brother to measure it to see how long it was. It was just under six feet. When Uncle Robert left, my brother started using the snake for a whip. After three or four times of trying to make the snake pop like a whip, eggs started coming out on every pop or two. We got eleven snake eggs from the snake. Yes, an egg battle was on, and we had fun. I don't remember who won. I don't think it matters.

I forgot to tell you about the hogs. The hogs were in the deal somehow: we were supposed to feed them and care for them. I'm talking about seventy-five hogs. There was a big pen over to the right of the barn, just off the side where the milk barn was. The hogs starting dying, and we did not know why. Dad called Mr. Burton, the owner, and told him about it. He called a veterinarian to come out and see what was wrong. It was sad news for all of us to hear that the hogs had hog cholera. And they all died. My dad and brother took the tractor and pond scoop to dig a hole big enough to bury the hogs. It took three long holes and two and a half days to get the job done . The smell was almost unbearable. We had to throw away the clothes we were wearing and take a bath every day. We were not going to take a chance on anything.

When we wanted to go all around the place, my brother and I would hook up the Ford tractor to the manure spreader. Everyone hopped up in the back, and off we'd go. We could take every wagon road around every field that we were cultivating, and it would take about an hour. This farm was 287 acres. Mr. Burton had bought another farm that joined this farm on the back side. It was 120 acres, but we did not work it. The Smith brothers had some kind of a deal on it.

The family had planed a fourth of July get-together, including cousins on both sides of the family. Families back then were large, anywhere from five to twelve children. Now you get the picture of how easy it was to fill up the manure spreader with kids and take off on a farm ride. We did just that. There had been a rain early in the week. It had mostly dried up, but the roads were still a little muddy in spots. On the way the kids were getting restless after seeing all the farm. One of them picked up a piece of a cow pie and threw the hard thing, hitting me upside of the head. I had been riding the tractor on the fender alongside my brother, who was driving the tractor. I was watching how he did everything so I could start learning how to drive. After I got hit, I hollered out, "Don't hit me anymore." My brother wanted to know what happened and as I told him, more cow pies were hitting both of us in the back and the head.

We had no weapons, but then it came to me; I told my brother to go through the muddy spots. The big cleats on the tires would bring up the mud, and I would use one hand to catch the mud, while holding on with the other hand. With my hand full of mud, I would hit the kids in the back of the manure spreader. This was working great, as my brother drove through every bit of mud he could find. Then a few of the kids starting crying, and my brother was trying to tell everyone to stop throwing things and settle down. Suddenly a big clunk hit my brother in the back of the head and forced him to lose control. We were going through a wooded area that had not dried out too much. My brother stepped on the brakes, and we slid into a cedar tree and broke off the headlight. There were one or two bent places on the tractor and on the front bumper.

When we got back to the house, we told Dad about the wreck. He said he would look at it after the relatives left. With everyone gone, Dad looked at the tractor. We told him how it had happened. Dad said we would have to pay for it. I was wondering how, with no money. Dad said he would buy the headlight, and we would have to put it on and straighten out the front bumper and give the tractor a wash. We agreed. Then Dad assigned extra work to us to pay for the damages. We were slaves, but we did not know it.

In the backyard between the chicken house and the house was a giant pear tree. Every year this tree had the largest pears, the sweetest pears that I had ever eaten. We canned the pears for preserves and pear halves. We kids would take a pear to school to have something for break to snack on. I was eating one of those pears, and a boy wanted a piece of it; I gave it to him. He wanted me to bring him a pear the next day, and I did. This turned out pretty good because he would bring me something and we would swap out. Then other kids wanted to get a pear, and I started selling the pears or swapping them. I often wished the tree would have pears all year long, because it was a moneymaker.

We had a little neighbor farmer next door just down the road. He was not much bigger than my older brother. He was a half-pint like my adopted grandma. My dad and the neighbor were rebuilding the fence that was on the property line. There was an old cow on the place that could jump the moon, just like in the nursery rhyme. We had to put a yoke around her neck so she could not jump any fences. Our neighbor had a field of clover hay that was eight to ten inches high all over the field; it was the prettiest green field around anywhere. The old cow was grazing the grass along the fence on a day-to-day routine. As the fence was built, they would tear out the old fence to where they were going to build for that day. Dad and the neighbor had strung the cattle fence, which was four feet tall. They were going to put two strings of barbed wire over the cattle wire.

The old cow would look over at the pretty clover while chewing on the grass she found along the fence. The neighbor had noticed the cow looking and made the remark, "Yeah, you old b----, you would like to be over in my field, wouldn't you?" Just about that time, the old cow took a step, threw her head up in the air as if standing on her back legs, and over the four-foot fence she went. Our neighbor went crazy and tried to catch the cow, but he could not. He got so mad he ran to the house and got his shotgun.

Still on the run, he was yelling, "I'll kill you." The cow started running, and he was running and shooting at the same time. The old cow made a turn and came back through the fence that had been torn down. When the neighbor got his breath back and they were building the fence again, my dad asked him if he would have killed the cow even if he had to pay for it. His reply? "Yes, I would; and if I had not run out of shells, I would shoot her now."

The second Christmas at this place, Mom baked my dad's favorite cake, peppermint candy cake. This cake became my favorite also.

Mr. Burton came by to see how everything was going. Mom offered him a piece of the cake with a cup of coffee. Mr. Burton got a piece of candy in his mustache, and my brother told him about it. After he left, we all made a joke about it. We said he was saving it for a treat later in the week.

Mr. Burton's little boy had come with him and was playing with our cat. The cat was a big yellow cat, full of energy all night long. He would sleep all day behind the kitchen stove, where it was warm. At night, he would roll a marble or a spool from thread all over the hard wood floor. He would make Dad mad, so he would get up and take the cat's toys away so he could go back to sleep.

Mr. Burton's son wanted the cat. Mr. Burton said he had some mice he wanted to catch at his house in town, and it would serve two purposes if the cat was given to his son. Mr. Burton could see in our eyes that we did not want to give up the cat. Mr. Burton said when the mice were caught, he would bring the cat back one day when his son was not paying attention to the cat. We all knew that was the last of our cat.

We soon found out that Dad would give away every last thing we had to please someone else, and our mom was not far behind him. I'll explain later.

The farm up the road back toward Deason had a jersey bull get out, and he headed our way. He could smell the cows coming in heat, and he jumped the fence, half tearing it down to get inside. Mr. Burton was visiting that day, and we were trying to drive the bull into the barn and put a rope on him. The bull had other ideas, though. After we got him in the barn, the owner of the bull showed up. The owner said he would put the rope on him, but he could not. So he said, "I'm going to grab his tail and hold him, while all of you put the rope on him." The owner of the bull put the bull's tail over his shoulder and lifted the bull's back feet off the ground. We were putting the rope on him when the tail slipped in the owner's hands. The bull jumped into a hole where a board was missing, and out the side of the barn he went. We ran him around the barn and finally cornered him and got the rope on him. The owner of the bull ran to his truck and backed it up to the loading chute. The bull was led up into the chute, but he did not want to go into the truck. He started kicking, snorting, blowing, and making all kinds of noises. He turned around in the chute and ran out.

Mr. Burton was trying to push from behind the bull; and when this happened, he turned and started running for the barn. Mr. Burton had an overcoat on, and it was sticking straight out behind him, just like when Grandpa was running from the sheriff. I knew right then that Grandpa's story was the truth. Mr. Burton reached the barn door and slipped through the door, sliding it shut before the bull had an opening to come in. The bull charged the barn door, butting it several times. We finally drove the bull around the barn into the old hogpen. We were trying to settle down the bull to where we could rope him again. The bull stood in the middle of the pen, legs apart, pawing the ground and snorting. We started into the fence and he would charge. When someone tried to go in from a different direction, he would charge. This bull was mad and dangerous.

I picked up some rocks, and I knew what kind to pick up. I threw a couple of warning shots to get his attention, and it did. I had to step inside the fence, and the bull was snorting and pawing the ground. I threw the rock as hard as I could and hit the bull in the nose. The bull went down to one knee. He came back up with blood running from his nose and just stood there. We all started to get the rope on him again, and this time he was led into the truck with no trouble. We looked at the bull's nose, and the part in between the sides of the nose was cut from one side to the other. I said, "I'm very sorry about it; I did not mean to do that much to the bull."

The owner said, "The bull had it coming, and I bet the bull won't try that again."

The owner wanted to know how I learned to throw rocks like that. He said, "I've never seen anything like it before." He thanked us and was on his way.

Then the grown-ups started getting on Mr. Burton about the overcoat. All were having a good laugh.

The neighbor below us, the one who was shooting at our cow, offered us kids a puppy when his dog had a litter. We begged our parents and got one of the puppies. The puppy was buff color and had a little white showing here and there on him. The puppy was a mixed breed, half Eskimo spit and half cocker spaniel. This little fellow did not know what a ride he was in for. The puppy would play a big part in the lives of six hungry children.

Chapter 10

Calvin's Farm

Well, it was time for Dad to put us on the move again. Every time we had things in order—I mean the bills paid and clothes on our backs and full-time employment—Dad would decide it was time to make a change. "It's not tough enough for us or something. It's time to run, I don't want success, I don't want to have money in my pockets." So my dad would say we've got to move. We did just that—again.

We moved to Spring Creek, my mom's fifth cousin's old farm. It was just past our old hometown of Tullahoma. We moved in and started school. My dad and Uncle Robert brought two mules and equipment. Uncle Robert, if you'll remember, is our adopted uncle. We called Mom's fifth cousin Uncle Calvin. Uncle Calvin had a lot of the equipment. Then my dad and Uncle Robert started getting ready for the spring planting. The biggest potato crop that we had ever planted was in the ground and looking good. The rest of the crops would be put in soon, and it would be time to take care of the garden for the season. Then it would be harvest time again.

The potatoes were sold in the field to beat some kind of law. This was the most money my dad ever had at one time. It was just over four thousand dollars. We still had to dig and bag the potatoes.

Dad got the money, and off he went somewhere. He had just bought an old car, and he left in it. Three or four days later he showed up, drunk and broke. Mom took him back without even much talking from my dad.

The garden came in, and Dad went and bought a truck. We started picking the vegetables and putting them on the truck, and then we went to town. We sold vegetables from house to house all over the town. Dad would go to the farmers' market and buy what we did not raise, and we continued to peddle the vegetables all summer long. This was big-time bucks. Dad would sleep all day Saturday while Uncle Robert, my older brother (who drove the truck without a license), and I went to sell the vegetables.

My dad would take off and get drunk whenever he felt like it. My older brother, being a family-minded person, quit school just after starting the ninth grade. He knew that Mom and the other brothers and sisters depended on him and Uncle Robert to pull us through.

My mom's brother moved into the house where Uncle Calvin moved out. My uncle was making moonshine whiskey not over a mile from our house. We moved into a bad place. My uncle drank and played cards all the time, so you know where all of our money went from all the hard work we all had done.

My mom's younger brother got into the peddling business. He knew we had a good corn crop, and he came by the farm to buy fifty dozen ears of corn. Dad priced them and he bought them, saying he would come back and pick them up. He came back and picked them up, and off he went. When the weekend came around, my uncle told my dad that we had shorted him three dozen corn.

Dad asked us about it. We all agreed there was no way that we miscounted the corn; we had counted the corn three times. Dad and my uncle argued. My father took a breather, an oil-bath air type breather for the truck, made of heavy metal, and hit my uncle in the head. It almost knocked him out, and he got up stumbling to his truck and left.

I gave my mom a scare. One day in school I was taking a test, and I told the boy in front of me to tell the teacher that I was sick. Don thought I was trying to cheat and would not tell the teacher anything. So I got up and started walking to the door of the classroom. I could hear the teacher calling me, but it sounded faraway. When the teacher got to me, he was mad. I started falling. The teacher, seeing that I was sick and falling, caught me before I hit the floor. If I had fallen, I could have tumbled down the stairs to the cafeteria entrance. I came to myself and got up where I had been lying on a table; they had put cold cloths on my head. One of the teachers carried me home, and Mom and Dad carried me to the doctor. I got checked out, and the doctor said it was an infection and I had fainted. The doctor gave me a shot and told me to go home and rest for two days before I got up and started running around again.

When I got back to school, I was ready for the makeup test. I studied the two days very hard, and I had an idea of the questions on the test. I wanted to pass this test really bad because I wanted to shove it up Don's nose. I took the test; and when I got it back, I was real proud of myself. The teacher stood in front of the class and showed the grade to the class, saying I had gotten 100 percent. The teacher also said, "This is what I want from each and every one of you." Was I proud! I was glad that I did not have to confront Don with it; he was already embarrassed. Don did not like being outdone. He was a spelling-bee champ for the county and went to the state and did well. He also was a baseball pitcher and was very good at that too.

All of this had come from running down a dirt gravel road barefoot, downhill and too fast for my little short legs to keep up with my body. I fell headfirst downhill and slid and scratched my kneecap, taking out a small hunk. Then about two weeks later, the infection had caused me to faint.

We were getting ready for supper one night and were ready to sit down at the table, when we all heard whining and whimpers coming from under the floor. We all said Mac—that was the name we had given to the puppy—was under the kitchen floor and couldn't get out. I went under the house and crawled as far as I could, called the puppy, and got him out. I washed up and ate, and everyone was happy—including the puppy.

But that was not the end of it. Two or three days later, Mac got hung up again and again could not get loose. Under the floor I called out to him, but Mac could not get loose and come to me. I went to the kitchen and talked to Mac and finally found the spot where he was under the floor. I had to take up some of the flooring to get him out. I also had to dig in the dirt around him to get Mac loose so I could pull him out. I spanked Mac and gave him a good talking-to. It must have worked, because this did not happen again.

Uncle Robert and my brother were doing most of the work nowadays. I helped until it was time for me to go to school. After school there was always something to do to help Mom. We kids—the ones that were big enough—had to take turns washing the dishes and cleaning up the kitchen. I started out standing on a box made of wood.

We boys were moving up in the world. We were sleeping on a cotton mattress. Our younger brother was growing up and outgrowing the weak kidney problem. We boys had to sleep on straw ticks while on the farm because the straw could be swapped out on a regular basis.

Mom and Dad went to town for some reason, and we kids had to take care of ourselves. My younger brother found a bottle of whiskey that Dad had hidden and drank it up and got drunk. He was funny. He would laugh awhile, he would cry awhile, he would hit the wall as hard as he could with his fist, he would then cry and laugh and blood was coming from his hand. My older brother settled him down, and we got him cleaned up. Finally he fell asleep.

With all the crops in and winter coming on, woodcutting was back in season. Uncle Robert and my brother did most of the cutting. Every weekend I would be helping haul the wood up. When enough wood was cut for our own use, they started cutting wood for sale and hauling it to town to sell it.

Looking back at the potato crop, what I hated the most about it was all the hard work we put in. Every morning there was dew on the plants. We had to dust the potatoes with poison for the bugs. We had to get up early, go dust with T.D.T., wash up, change clothes, eat breakfast, and run to catch the bus for school. This was work! Almost five areas of taters is a lot of taters.

We often called this place Spring Creek because we can remember the swimming hole. We could only go swimming on the hottest days of summer because the water was so cold. It was so cold that it would raise chill bumps on your arms; if you were in the water too long, you would turn blue until it became unbearable and you had to get out of the water. We rode the mules down the hill that was almost too steep to climb. Going downhill, we would slide up to our hands, which were holding onto the mane. My brother was on the lead mule, and I followed on the little mule. These mules were named Pete and Dan. Going back up the hill was just as hard. We had to hold on with our legs and hands and lie forward on the mule's neck, taking the hill at a fast pace to make it to the top without falling off. Boy, was this living! We loved being cowboys and riding, and would act out a movie every once in a while on the mule's back, like riding off into the sunset.

Along toward the end of summer, Mom got my aunt, her family, and all of us kids to go to the creek for a swim. We all were enjoying the water, and it was cold as usual. After about an hour in the water, I came out to warm up. I was standing behind the women, who blocked the wind from me. My aunt did not like this for some reason; I don't know why. Suddenly my aunt grabbed me by the shoulders and shoved me toward the creek, and into the creek I went. When I tried to get out, she shoved me back in the creek. We were all having fun, and the other kids were laughing about my aunt playing around with us kids.

Everything settled down, and everyone was in and out of the water at intervals for warming up every so often. I moved around and caught my aunt off guard. I grabbed her by the waist and lowered my shoulder, and to the creek I went with her. I tried to stop but could not. My aunt had hold of me and was holding on and would not let go. Into the water we went. My aunt was screaming and yelling and cursing. "The little devil" and some more choice words came out of her nasty mouth. Then my aunt said, "I've got my period, and I have to go four more days now," and a few more choice words came out for me. She came out of the water and was going to whip me, but my mom stepped in and said, "No, you don't. The kids don't know what you are talking about. You are the one that started playing with the kids, and you got what was coming to you." I did not know what she was talking about. I know that nowadays kids at my age could write a book on sex education, but I knew nothing.

Going back to the house, I was thankful for my mom being there. My mother and father would protect their offspring. Then it hit me why my aunt shoved me in the water. This was payback for the well water trick that I had pulled on her at the other farm. My uncle and aunt moved in just below us. The feeling was mutual between us: we just didn't like each other. I cannot like a cheater, liar, stealer, crook, or a lazy person. This I knew from an early age, and it is still with me today.

Every once in a while we would get the privilege of going to town to see a movie. My older brother would drive the old model-A car to the edge of town and park it, and we would walk about three miles to the movie at the Marshall Theater. Cowboy movies were shown every Saturday morning, along with a cartoon, a chapter series, a newsreel, and advertisements for a thin dime. We boys would have a quarter, and that would buy a bag of popcorn and a candy bar as well as get us into the movies. We would come home and act out every part of the movie. Sometimes there would be a double feature, and this was both a treat and a bargain. When the movie was over, we never looked forward to the long walk back to where the old car was. Parking here kept my brother from getting a ticket for not having a driver's license.

Our grandpa would go to movies with us every once in a while. We would have to wait on him at the bootlegger's to get his drink of whiskey and visit with the women. Grandpa did not like to buy whiskey from his son. Grandpa always insisted on going by the women's place of business. Every once in a while, we boys would have to knock on the door and tell Grandpa to hurry up or we would be late for the movie.

Once we got to the movies, Grandpa would go to sleep. By the time he slept through the double feature, a cartoon, the newsreel, and a chapter series, he got about three and a half hours of sleep. When the movie was over, we would have to wake up our grandpa. We would say, "Wake up; the movie is over."

Grandpa would say, "Shut up, son, I'm listening to the pretty music."

There was no music playing, and the theater was empty except for us boys and Grandpa.

The children at school all played marbles. I liked the different colors and took a fancy to the marble game. Somehow I traded for some marbles and started playing. I could see there was more to the marble-shooting game than it looked like. I watched and

learned how to play the games. I asked my dad how to play and
to teach me how to hold the marble and shoot it. He knew. Dad
said his cousin was the best around anywhere when he was a
boy. I practiced and practiced some more and was getting better
each and every day. Then I went to the game where you put three
marbles from each player into the center and the winner is the
one that shoots out more marbles than anyone else. If I shot it
out, I got to keep it.

Soon I was getting more and more marbles and began trading
the marbles for things and money. I was in business, and it felt
good. I did not tell Dad about the money, or he would have taken
it from me. At the end of the school year, I had a flour sack full
of marbles. This flour sack would hold ten pounds of flour. This
meant ten pounds of marbles, and was I proud of myself. I loved
all of the different colors. The cat's-eye marbles were not out yet,
or I would have turned a double backflip.

The money we made all summer long from peddling and from the
farm was gone. We were to start back to school shortly, and there
was no money. We needed new shoes, britches, shirts, and coats
for school. Dad asked Uncle Robert for the money, saying he'd
pay him back real soon. Uncle Robert knew my dad was lying. If
my dad got paid in town, it never made it home; he always found
a way to leave it in town. My mom knew this about him, but
would not admit it.

My dad went off pouting, and then my mom asked for the
money. Uncle Robert answered the same: he had no money. Mom
knew better and started worrying the old man and wringing her
hands. She said, "I don't know what we are going to do. The kids
don't have clothes, and they need to go to school." Finally after
about three days, Uncle Robert gave the money to Mom.

Chapter 11

White's Farm

Halfway through the winter, we moved again. This time it was to be White's Farm. This place was farther out to the other side of the county. The house was log and badly in need of a lot of repairs. The house had steps in front and no porch. To the left was Mom and Dad's room and a big open room where the heater stove was. The kitchen was in back all the way across the back of the house. The big table barely fit in the room; and it's a good thing that Dad had made wooden benches for us kids to sit on, because there was not very much room left to get around the table. Before you went into the kitchen, to the right of the door was a set of stairs that went upstairs to the boys' room. I can remember lying in bed and looking up at the stars through the holes in the tin roof. The roof was so steep that the rain ran off without leaking.

Uncle Robert had a little building out back with one large room, no heat or plumbing, and no lights. The extra room in this little building would be the bathhouse, where the men could take a bath. This was used mostly in the summer months and only on Saturday or special occasions if any.

The dog came with us, and he sniffed everything in sight and ran around until he was exhausted. Weekends were cutting wood for use and for selling. This kept all of us busy until spring planting season. Then the same old thing: planting corn, cotton, a big garden, and lots of potatoes.

We started back to the Center Grove School, the mean school that we went to earlier. The school had many improvements. They had bathrooms now and a lunchroom. The school had a new principal, who would paddle you in a heartbeat, as you will read.

We started school as soon as we got settled in. We missed about a week. I was in the seventh grade, but still had not grown much in height.

We had a spelling test once a week of twenty-five words. I could not spell. I was making bad grades, and I did not want to fail. I had to put in more work and learn how to spell. I did not know how to study to learn how to spell. I knew that writing the words twenty times was supposed to help. This was what I tried to do every week, but I did not have time to do all that writing. So I had to learn how to spell. I wrote the words out ahead of time, before I missed them on the next test. The day of the test came, and I was ready. The teacher and the principal, one and the same, started giving out the words and I began spelling. About the fifth word was given, and I put it down on paper. It felt good, and I must have smiled. The teacher started watching me, and the more I spelled the more I was grinning. Then the principal came over to me and asked, "Are you cheating?"

"No, sir."

He started looking in my desk, at my hands, on the back of my paper, and everywhere else he could look. We finished, and the papers were graded. I made 100 percent. The principal got so mad, he called me up front and paddled me. While I was bent over and the paddle was doing its thing, I got as close to the desk as I could. The paddle hit the desk and my bottom at the same time and broke. I hollered real loud, like I was hurting big time. The principal stopped the paddling and asked if I was okay. I faked a little, rubbed my bottom, and limped back to my desk. The other kids were so quiet one could hear a pin drop on the floor.

When school was out, he said for me to stay after class and I did. He said, "I'm going to let you take the test over again." I took the test over again and passed it with another 100 percent score.

While he was paddling me, I could not feel a thing; I had my mind fixed on the perfect grade in spelling and I felt nothing but good. The principal said he was sorry and that he would make it up to me. He even apologized for accusing me of cheating. I told him I did not cheat or lie or steal. We became best friends. He had an Irish setter that was a show dog and a breeder; he brought the dog to school every day. I took him on walks and fed him every now and then.

I kept up my spelling and the other subjects and passed without any difficulties. I was cut from a play because I was so far off-key when singing. It was funny to me when the teacher finally figured out who the bad key was. I knew all the time. He gave me something else to do; I don't remember what.

Coming home from school one spring day, my younger brother was looking at everything and dragging his feet. I told him Dad told us to come home as fast as we could get there because we had to help with the work. He kept dragging his feet, and I was asking him to come on and he would not. I had some of those old kitchen matches in my pockets for starting fires in the stoves when it was my turn to build the fires. I told my brother, "I will put this match to your butt if you don't come on."

He was as big as, if not taller than, I was, and he didn't pay any attention to me . I struck the match, and while it was still fizzing, I stuck the match to his butt on the bottom of the overall britches. It burned a hole through the britches; and before I could stop it, it burned a hole in his butt. He jumped up and down screaming and crying, and then the race was on. He had dropped his books, and I had to pick them up before I could start to run to catch up with him.

My brother beat me to the house by a quarter of a mile. I have never seen him run so fast. I have never heard him scream so loud either. I got a whipping; Mom whipped me real good. It was worth it, though, because from that time on when I asked him to hurry up, he did.

The whole family was in the field for cotton picking. Mom brought an old quilt with her and put it on the ground for the girls and my youngest brother to play on while she was picking cotton. This worked out real good. The field started to change colors, from white to dark brown, the color of cotton stalks and dirt. My dad saw that and knew that all the cotton would be picked before it was ruined in the field.

Two days later, my dad said, "I'm going to the house and fix something on the old truck. I'll take the youngest son with me."

Mom said okay.

It was about one o'clock when Dad left. Mom asked Uncle Robert to tell her when it got to five o'clock, because she would have to quit and go fix supper. Five o'clock came, Mom left, and the rest of the pickers stayed in the field and picked up to almost dark. When we got to the house and found out what Dad had done, we could not believe it, but we knew it was true. Dad left us in the field. He did not have fixing the truck on his mind at all. He had fried chicken on his mind. When he got to the house, he told my youngest brother to feed the chickens and get them real close so he could catch one of the frying size, and he did. He killed, cleaned, and plucked the chicken and got it ready for the frying pan. He built the fire up in the kitchen stove and fried the chicken. There were biscuits left from breakfast, and they just needed to be heated up in the oven. My dad and youngest brother ate the whole chicken and the biscuits. This frying size chicken would dress out at about two pounds.

When Mom got to the house, Dad was in bed taking a nap. He was just getting up because Mom had awakened him coming into the house. Mom's fussing at him did not bother him a bit. Dad said he did not feel good after he ate the chicken and had to lie down. Uncle Robert and we boys had a little joke that Dad did not hear. The joke was, "If I ate that much chicken, I would feel sick too." I can say without doubt of any kind that Dad did not care one way or the other, as long as he got his way and got out of any work that he could.

Crops were in, cotton was sold and in the barn, and it was back to cutting wood. Dad would take a load and sell it as fast as we could cut it.

Somehow I got a little spare time and built two rabbit traps. I think it was that Dad liked fried rabbit, and any food that anyone else put on the table was food that he did not have to put on the table. These rabbit traps, if successful, would help him out. I could remember exactly how Grandpa built the traps. These traps looked good. I had to handsaw all of the boards out of old boards that were in the barn loft. It was a lot of work, but I did not mind because I had catching rabbits on my mind. I finished and set off to the woods to find the best spot I could to set the traps. I knew what kind of little trail to pick; Grandpa had showed me and explained what to look for under the thick undergrowth. I put a wedge of an apple in each box trap, back toward the back of the trap. I had to check them every morning and every night. I did, and I was catching rabbits—two and sometimes three a week. I was a big hunter and provider. The trick to catching rabbits was to keep moving the traps around. Grandpa said the rabbits stay in a small area and don't want any other strange rabbits coming into their area. So I kept moving the traps around and kept catching the rabbits.

One night after supper, we were sitting around the living room stove. We were listening to the grown-ups talking. My brother was in the kitchen washing and drying the dishes. We had to take turns, that is, the two oldest had to at this time. Then a thought jumped in my head. I asked my mom, "Mom, if I catch three rabbits in the morning, will you let me out of doing the dishes when it comes my turn?"

Mom said, "No, you have four or five traps."

Dad told her, "No, just two traps. Are you afraid to bet him?"

This little shove got Mom to say, "Okay, then. You have got to catch three rabbits."

I said yes, and off to bed I went. I knew morning always comes early on a farm.

I got up and dressed and out the door before breakfast. I was checking the traps early. The first trap was triggered. I checked and real carefully I ran my hand down in the trap and grabbed the hind legs of the rabbit and closed the door on the trap. Back at the house, I showed the rabbit to my mom. Since I was not big enough, I told Dad to kill the rabbit, and I set off to the woods again. I checked the same trap, but nothing else was in there. I went to the next trap and checking it the same way, pulled out a rabbit and closed the door. With the rabbit secured in my grip, I opened the trapdoor again just a little. I could see eyes looking at me. I set the trap back on the ground. I was off to the house again with the number two rabbit. I gave it to my dad, and off I went again. I caught the hind legs of the rabbit and pulled him out of the trap. The whole time I was reaching down in the box, I was thinking of what had happened to my grandpa; I certainly did not want to mess up my britches. Well, I got back to the house and gave the rabbit to my dad.

After the jumping and jerking stopped, I took him from my dad and laid him on the pile. I looked at Mom and said, "Look, Mom, I got three rabbits." She got mad and started cussing and saying I tricked her and I had more traps in the woods than just the two. I told her if she could find more than two traps in the woods, that I would wash the dishes for two weeks by myself. I made up my mind I was not going to wash those dishes when it came my turn. She would have to beat me to death. I'm glad it did not come to that. Mom washed the dishes and fussed the whole time. Mom stayed mad at me for a long time. Sometimes I think Mom never did get over it; she hated to lose at anything, even playing card games.

Spring was here, and it was planting time again. School was almost over with for another year, and I passed again.

With planting done and no money coming in, Dad left Uncle Robert on the farm to take care of it; he could cut wood and do the chores while we worked at the nursery. Yes, Dad got us two oldest boys a job at the nursery and we all went to work every day just like men. There was a little store on the route to and from work. Every Friday we would stop and get a coke, candy bar, or bag of peanuts, and sometimes an oatmeal cake. That was payment for the boys' work for this week of work, paid in full. Dad collected our wages, and we never saw the money. This was all summer long.

Later in life I figured out why Dad wanted Uncle Robert to stay on the farm. He did not want Uncle Robert to find out how much money he could make at the nursery. Dad would give Uncle Robert some money to keep him in chewing tobacco and a little pocket change, and that was it. Dad was securing his free labor source. Dad knew he had full control over his boys.

We boys still had the treat of seeing a movie every once in a while. My older brother would drive to the edge of town, just like before, and park the truck; we would walk the rest of the way to the movies. This old truck was worn out, and we had to park it on a hill and let it roll off to get it started. Dad finally traded it for a bigger truck.

The crops had been gathered, including the cotton picking, and the money was in the pocket. We thought everything was good, but it must not have been. Dad said, "We are moving."

"Where?" the kids asked all at once.

Dad said Georgia, and off we went to another place to make our home. I hate to move, I know it now. I'm not going to forget it again.

Chapter 12

Gene's Chicken Farm

We got to Georgia, and the house was a lot newer than expected and in better shape. It was smaller than what we needed, but it would do. It was the best house we ever lived in. Dad said, "Come on, I'm going to show you the chicken houses." When we saw the huge chicken houses, our eyes were so big. There were two bigger ones, each of which held five thousand chickens; one held four thousand; and Dad was to repair the other house to hold thirty-five hundred. Then it hit me: we were going to be chicken farmers. Our new jobs were to feed the chickens and make sure that water was running and the drinking pans were clean. The water was automatic. But we had to feed, and this meant opening the feed sack up and putting the feed out by hand.

Dad's cousin owned this chicken farm; and until money started coming in on a regular basis from the sale of frying-size chickens, things were going to be tight. So off to the woods again we all went and started cutting pulpwood, which was a lot easier than firewood, except for the pine sap, which had to be cut off the saws with gasoline on a regular basis.

Mac made the trip too. He was a fine dog, and the whole family loved him very much.

We started school, and it was different down here. The kids didn't seem as smart as the kids of Tennessee. The school was easier. The homework was lighter. This was going to be a breath of fresh air for me. The kids took smoke breaks out behind the shop building. They stood around and traded cards that had pictures of cars on them. They traded everything: marbles, baseball cards, matches, and smokes. The trading cards came from buying bubble gum.

The chickens in the houses were doing just fine, and it was getting near time to catch and haul them to market. One night just at dark, a big truck pulled up to the chicken houses. The chickens' cages were stacked real high up on the truck. Some of them hung out over the front of the truck, over the cab. The crew of four came out of the truck. There were three chicken catchers and the driver, who was the boss. The lights were turned out in the chicken house. This was strange to me. *How are they going to catch chickens in the dark?* When the lights went out, the chickens bunched up real close together. Then came the fun. The chicken catcher went toward the chickens and dropped to one knee and started grabbing one leg of each chicken. When he stood up, he had sixteen chickens, eight in each hand. This was something to see for a young boy like me.

I wanted to try it. My hands were too small, though, and I was not strong enough to pull and swing the chickens. The most I could get was eight, which was four chickens in each hand. I thought that was good for the first time I tried to catch chickens.

The chicken cages were filled with chickens and loaded one at a time until the truck was completely full and there was no more room. The truck left—and here came another truck. We started catching and loading it. One house was finished, and we started on another. Dad said we should be finished in about an hour.

"What time is it?" I asked.

"It's twelve thirty in the morning. You go tell your mom we will be at the house in one and a half hours, and she should have something to eat for all of us."

Off I went on the run. I knew this was easier work than catching chickens and loading them. I was getting tired, because I had been up all day and gone to school. I was thinking *I won't have to go to school tomorrow*. I went into the house on the run and told my mom what Dad said about something to eat. Mom looked at me and said, "Get out of here. You stink, and you've got chicken s---- all over you."

I was so caught up in the excitement that I had not even noticed. When you drop to one knee and move the chickens around, it makes them go to the bathroom. When you pick them up, it is usually on you—all down the front of your britches. I chalked this up as a good experience for me. I was learning and adding common-sense thoughts in my head and it might help me out somewhere in my life. I didn't mind. But I knew for sure I didn't want to be a chicken rancher for the rest of my life.

We made it through the winter. This was a hard winter for north Georgia. The grown-ups were talking about it. They said there had been more days of freezing weather than they had had in years. I don't think Dad liked the chicken rancher thing either. The weather broke, and It would be turning spring in a short while. Dad was getting restless feet again. Then, as my Mom would say, right out of the blue, we were going to move again. This we did again and again and over and over again. We were off, and where to I didn't know. We were all together, and that was all that mattered to me.

Chapter 13

Shahan's Rock Creek Place

For some reason, I can't remember ever pulling out in the daylight when moving. We were off, and I was in the back of the truck. There were two brothers back there too. We started going up the mountain, and it sure was beautiful with all the hills. You could see the bare rocks among the trees, because there were no leaves on the trees. It was still beautiful to look at. Now, riding backward in the truck with the sun up, in your eyes if going forward, it was like a flashlight when we were looking out the back of the truck. It would light the hidden valleys and the top of the hills on the side of the mountain—and what a sight for young people to see.

Dad stopped up on the mountain at an old store. He went in the store and got a bunch of food. He told Mom to fix all of us a sandwich. Mom did, and it was a bologna and cheese with mayonnaise. We stayed hungry; all of us that worked all the time were always hungry. We brought our own water; cokes were out of the question when it came to nine soda pops at once. Dad would have screamed like a mashed cat trying to pay for that many at one time. The move was going just fine, and I had heard Mom and Dad talking while we were eating. They said that in about two and a half hours we would be there. Neither said where; sometimes I think they did not know either. They just drove until they found a house empty, and we would hop off the truck and fill up the empty house instantly.

We finally arrived at the house. We were tired from riding so long in the back of the truck. We starting unloading the truck, and soon everything was inside. I recently asked my older brother about moving—how long did it take to load up or unload? I expected it took a couple hours. But my brother said, "Hell, it only took about thirty minutes; we did not have very much of anything back in those days."

I can remember the old house in every detail. It had a high wraparound porch, L-shaped and about six feet off the ground at the highest point. The living room was large, with a big fireplace. It had three bedrooms. The kitchen was not big but it was efficient, and the kitchen table where we all ate was there on the right side as you walked into the kitchen from the living room. The back porch was a little smaller than the front but was L-shaped also. Coming in the house from the front door, the fireplace was on the left and the hallway was just beyond. Down the short hallway, Mom and Dad's room was on the left. On down the hall, all of us boys and Uncle Robert had one room, which was to the left, and the girls' room was to the right.

I knew this house was here, because all of the people working the nursery would take shelter here when there came rain or a storm. I knew what was in store for us—back to work at the nursery.

This place had a huge garden spot of about one and a half acres. We planted everything we could and in every spot that was open.

We started to school back in town. I would have to take gym classes. I really did not know what this meant. I had been going to schools that had one or two rooms only. The school in Georgia had one classroom and had shops of some kind. I had never taken the time to find out what they were.

I walked into gym class, and we all sat in the bleachers. The roll call came, and I was introduced to the class as the new boy. The coach said, "Go get dressed and get back on the court in five minutes."

Everyone jumped up. I followed them downstairs, and everyone was getting naked and putting on some kind of little short pants and tennis shoes. These boys were taking off more clothes than I had ever seen before. They pulled off T-shirts and little white shorts called drawers. I went back upstairs and sat on the bleachers. I did not know what to do. Soon the coach came by and asked, "Why are you not dressed and ready to play?"

I answered, "I don't have the clothes. No one told me what I would need to have for gym."

He got mad at me. Then I told him I had never been to a school that had a gym. I told him that all of my schools were way out in the country. The coach said, "Get your things this weekend and be ready to play next week, okay?"

I went home and told Mom about it. Mom rounded up some money from somewhere, and we went to town and got the shorts, tennis shoes, T-shirts, and the regular drawers. That's the kind you wear everywhere every day, all-the-time kind of drawers. When I got to school, I had a paper bag full of the stuff and carried it around all day. When I got to gym class, I asked the coach which locker I would have. He assigned me a locker, and I slipped out of my britches and into the gym shorts without pulling off the regular shorts. I was not ashamed of my body. I had never been naked in front of a big bunch of boys or anyone else before. We had always turned our backside to get dressed—it was the way we were taught.

I was glad this was the last period of the school day. When all the boys were showering, I was watching and learning what the

shower was all about. This was going to be a first for me. My baths
all had been in the number-three iron-galvanized tub.

I waited until everyone had gotten out of the shower. Then I
went in the shower, and this was a treat to me. It was a lot easier
than the tub. Then I thought, *I'm sure glad I watched the other boys
first because I forgot to bring a bath towel.* I also forgot—because
I did not know—that there were special socks called gym socks
to wear with the tennis shoes. I was learning fast, and everything
was getting better, I thought. When we went swimming, we wore
cutoff blue jeans.

We had to walk or hitch a ride to school. I saw a girl from one of
my classes one day just across the creek going toward town. Her
name was Edna, and we became friends. She told me if I got down
there before she left for school that her dad or her brother would
give me a ride to school.

The garden work was done after school and on the weekends. It
was a big garden, and we had plenty of potatoes planted. They had
to be DDT'd early in the morning, and I had to do it. My job was
to help with the garden and around the house until school was out.
My dad, Uncle Robert, and my older brother were working at the
nursery; and the brother next-younger than me would be starting
to work at the nursery as well as soon as school was out. We started
off this year working as scratchers in June budding peach trees. My
Dad was a budder. My brother and Uncle Robert worked elsewhere
at the nursery.

My younger brother and I were scratchers. This meant a nine-
and-one-half-hour day. The work was done mostly with us being
down on our knees. Down on our knees and bent over, with our
heads just off the ground. The budders were placing the buds
about three or four inches off the ground on the side of the peach
seedling. Then a wrap was put around the bud to hold it in place
until it grew onto the tree. When the ground got dried out and
very dusty, the dust would come up from the dried dirt when we

blew our breath on the ground. After a rain it would be muddy, and the steam from the ground would be coming up in our faces. The scratcher's job was to pull the dirt out from between the little seedlings. Pulling out the grass, and pruning the limbs off the seedlings. The limbs had to be pruned about five inches high off the ground. This work was hard on everyone's knees and backs. The hidden rock under the surface was murder on tender, sore knees. Every year the budders and wrappers had to get used to the pain. The knees would have to get tough, and everyone would have to work through the pain and the sore knees.

The man that owned the nursery was a hard man to work for. He wanted the work done his way. The older son wanted the work done his way. The younger son wanted the work done his way. It was very confusing at first, but then we had it figured out. We talked to the younger son, our boss, about it. We asked, "Is it okay if we do the work the way you want it done until your dad or brother show up? And then we do the work the way they want it done, and when they leave we go back to the way you want it done?"

The boss said, "That is okay with me." This made the young boss feel good, because it let him know that we liked the way that he wanted the work done.

After the nursery owner and the older son left after a visit one day, we had only about thirty minutes work left in the day. The men started talking, and my dad said, "You know, boss, we never have done anything for your father."

All of the men agreed, "That is right." No one could ever remember anything that was ever done for the owner of the nursery.

My dad said, "With about seven minutes to go before the end of the workday, why don't we all give the owner the last five minutes of work to show our appreciation for him?"

Again, all the men agreed, "That is a good idea, and let's do it."

The young boss agreed that we had never done anything for his father. He said, "Why not? Let's do it."

All of the men and the boys got up and called it a day and were walking out of the field. Everyone was happy. It was payday, and being Friday meant two days of not being down on our sore knees.

The following week the men were talking and asking, "Do you think we can do it again this week?" They were looking at my dad for the answer because it was his deal.

My dad said, "We will try again Friday, but we will ask for fifteen minutes this time."

All the men agreed, and everyone started waiting for Friday to be here soon.

Friday was here, and there were thirty minutes to go to the end of the day. My dad said, "Everyone liked it so much last week giving your father five minutes; why don't we give him fifteen minutes today? How about it?" my dad said to the young boss.

While the young boss was thinking, the other men said, "That is a good idea." Everyone said, "I'm in," one after the other.

The young boss said, "Why not?"

We all got up with fifteen minutes to go and walked out of the field. Everybody was laughing and talking and lined up to get their paychecks.

The following week the men were going to do it again. Dad said for one of the other men to take the lead and everyone would join in with him. The worker said, "Let's give the boss another five minutes today."

The young boss said we were giving up too much time to his father and wanted to know why. All of the men knew then that they had gone to the well once too often. The intervals were too close together and too often, and this made the young boss suspicious. The young boss started counting and calculating, using his hand for counting and figuring out the numbers. The men were thinking, "Say something; he is about to figure it out."

Several men had inputs, but the boss said, "I'll be damned. You all have not given my father a damn thing."

Everyone started laughing. The young boss joined in on the laughing. He said, "The joke is on me, and you men have got me real good." Jokes went back and forth, teasing the young boss. After taking some time to think about it, the young boss said, "Let's keep this to ourselves. If this gets out, my father will want you all to make this work up." Then the young boss said, "I don't want to make it up either, because I don't want to give the old man anything either."

One of the men spoke up and said, "If the old man found out, he might take it out of your hide." Everyone had a good laugh, and it was a fun day that day. Going to the house, our dad reminded us boys to keep our mouths closed. Dad said, "The owner and the older brother would raise hell with the young boss if they found out what had taken place."

After June budding, we worked at almost anything that needed to be done. We were cutting grass, pulling weeds, hoeing and chopping small grass out of the rows of the trees and cutting the grass loose, until harvest time came for the trees to be dug up and balled up for market. We finished the shade tree field down in the creek bottom. We were glad to finish because this was a sweat hole and there was no air to be had down under the trees. We went to another field and started to clean it up. At the end of the rows was a corncob pile. The cobs had been dumped out in a huge pile. They had soaked up rain and were heavy. We were so happy being out of the creek bottom where no air was stirring and it had been hot and sticky work for three weeks. Someone threw a cob, I just don't remember who. The corncob battle was on. The young boss got in on it because he had no choice.

All of the kids and the young men age twenty and under took part in the corncob battle, including the young boss. The "old man," the owner of the nursery, was on the prowl in his Buick. He drove up without anyone seeing him. Then the young boss got hit upside of the head. It was a solid hit, and he stumbled backward a little bit, rubbing where it hurt. The owner hollered out, "Hot damn, hit the son-of-a-gun again."

We did not know the owner was around, and we all froze in our tracks and looked to see what was coming next. The owner asked his son if the cob had knocked some damn sense in his head. The owner was having fun and laughing about it. We all joined in on the laughing as the son was rubbing the side of his head and laughing with the rest of us. The owner said, "No more throwing; someone might get hit in the eye or get hurt." Then he said, "It was worth every penny just to see my son hit upside of the head. Let's get back to work now."

After the old man left, the young boss said, "If I had not got hit upside of the head, he would have fired me."

The question came from someone in the group, "Why don't he like you?"

The young boss said, "He likes me, but when I disagree with him, he gets mad. It's his way or no way."

This work kept up all summer long, and the garden was coming in and Mom was wanting to get to canning. This meant the cleaning of the fruit jars. My younger brother and I had to wash the jars, which were called mason jars. We had to draw the water from the well and fill up the number-three tub and a number two with water. One was for washing; the other tub was for rinsing. We washed and rinsed the whole weekend. We washed again the following weekend. It seemed like I had washed fruit jars for days on end, and my hands had never been cleaner. My hands looked like wrinkled-up prunes. Mom explained when we complained about it, that we were going to fill every fruit jar we had if we had enough stuff to fill them up—and that we would be proud of ourselves when we all had plenty to eat come winter.

Mom got in touch with my adopted grandma and asked her if she wanted to help out with the canning. She did. The work went a lot easier with Grandma to talk to. Mom bought some peaches from town, and they canned them too. Mom had to buy some more fruit jars, and Grandma brought all she had and all she could round up. You know what this meant—more jar washing for me and my brother.

When Grandma left, she had a pickup truck half full of canned goods of all kinds. I was going to miss her again, because she was funning all the time about something and making everyone within earshot laugh.

Grandpa moved back in and started working at the nursery. I did not mind a bit, because when Uncle Robert or Grandpa lived with us, they got up early and built the fires. Otherwise, my older brother and I had to take turns. Our parents somehow did not think it was their duty to get up and build the fires. Our dad was going to town more often now for some reason. He would have some kind of a whiskey bottle around every weekend. My grandpa would go to town every weekend and have a drink or two, but we never saw him real drunk. He was not wild with it. He would just come home and ask my mom to fix him a bite to eat; and then he'd go to bed.

Grandpa would wake up the next morning like nothing had ever happened. He was coming home one day early and was carrying something in his arms. We boys were out in the front yard and saw him coming up the road. He started falling forward and leaned toward the front; his legs were trying to stay in front of him, but that was not happening. He fell and slid on the gravel road, but he got up and started walking again. The same thing happened again. We boys were laughing about it and ran to Grandpa and helped him to the house. He was all skinned up and bleeding on his elbows and one hand. He was carrying ten pounds of ocean perch fish. He had a skinned place on his nose. That gravel is tough on the skin, I know this so well.

Chapter 14

Moving On

I started school again, and everything was going pretty good, I thought. I was a little more interested in the subjects that I was signing up for. Mom finally convinced Dad that I had to start dressing a little better, or she started buying better clothes—anyway, something happened. I still had the poor look, but it was better than it had been.

All of a sudden, Dad said we had to move again—and so we did. We threw a bunch of clothes in the truck and hit the road. My older brother, Dad, and I were on the road going to find out about a job in Maryland. I had never heard of Maryland. Where was Maryland? How far was Maryland? Dad did not know, but he had a road map and money for gas and food. We had a camper top on the back of the truck to sleep in while we were on the road. Dad said the name of the nursery was Bountiful Ridge Nursery. "It's in Princess Ann, Maryland." And Dad kept driving.

While going up the road and getting farther away from the house, I was thinking *I'll miss the old place.* That summer Dad would take us boys down on the river on weekends to fish. We would set trout lines and camp out on the weekends. There was plenty of fish caught, and there was plenty of fun. Then Dad said, "Let's invite all the kinfolks for a fish fry on the fourth of July." And we did—his cousin, Mom's cousins, but mostly on my dad's side of the family. We went around to anyone who did not have a ride and loaded them up on the truck, and my brother drove them to the river. There were thirty-four people on the truck at one time, if I remember right. My brother had a very small opening in the windshield to look through, and I don't know how he did it without having an accident, but he did. This was just one of the good times that the old place provided for all of us.

The countryside was so breathtaking everyplace I looked. Up through east Tennessee and all of the mountains. Beautiful houses, barns, and the stock in the fields grazing everywhere. We only stopped to get food and to go to the bathroom. We stretched our legs and were on the go again. Dad parked just off the main highway in a little spot that looked like a pull-off area. We had gotten stuff at a store to fix sandwiches and had plenty of water to drink and wash our hands. We ate and crawled up in the back of the truck to sleep the night away. I was to fall asleep real fast. It was just getting dark as we lay down. I tossed and turned, and Dad and my brother were getting on me. "Settle down, boy, and get some sleep." About the time I fell asleep, a big air horn blasted out loud, and I almost jumped out of the truck.

There was a side road not far down the road from where we were. The next morning, I saw skid marks in the road and on the side road. That's what the loud air horn was blowing at last night—the car must have pulled out in front of the truck. The big air horn had sounded like it was outside the truck camper right on top of us. Dad said that sound carries farther in the dark and will sound a lot louder than it really is.

We were driving through Virginia and taking in all the sights, and we thought it was a beautiful state. My brother and I pointed out different things, like how big the farmhouses were and the white fences. We all said, "These people must be rich and have everything to waste money on a fence like that." The road was up one hill and down another, up another hill and then down, and on and on this went like a roller coaster. I can remember one stretch of the highway where one could see about ten miles straight ahead. This road had the up and down hills in it. I could see the tops of each hill until they ran together as one. We drove on and were trying to get to the big hill, and we drove and drove. That ten-mile stretch of road turned into about thirty miles of up and down. When we started to climb up the big long hill and saw that that this was the hill that we saw miles back down the road, it was almost an unbelievable sight.

There was a store at the top, and we stopped and got something to eat and to take a break. While we were eating, we looked back down the road, and it was the same look from the other end. This was on the old road, long before the interstate roads were built. While writing this, I was thinking of how much beauty was taken out of the country with the building of the interstate highways. I know, "but everyone gets there faster." That is right, but when you are poor, you will always have more time than you have money.

Dad was driving along, and the sign said the bridge was up ahead. The Chesapeake Bay Bridge—and what a bridge it was. We boys had never seen anything like this before, and it was huge. Our eyes took in everything, from the water down below to the high rails of the bridge, boats on the water, birds in the air and perching on the bridge. For two young boys to see this was greater than anything that we had ever seen before. I knew this sight would stay with me for a long time.

We looked at the map, and Dad said that in about three hours, we would be getting close—and we were. We started down the road that led to the nursery. Dad said according to the map, after making the turn we only had about five or six more miles. About the time we were thinking we might be lost, we saw a black man getting out of his car in his yard. We stopped and asked where the Bountiful Ridge Nursery was. The man started talking, and we had never heard such before. He said, "You go down the road about a mile and a half. There will be a big patch of woods on the left. Turn left before the woods, and then go about one mile up the dirt road." We thanked him and were on our way again. Dad drove up and went inside. He stayed about an hour; and when he came back out, he said we all had jobs. Now to find a house. We went back to town and made inquiries. Dad finally said, "I found one, and it's back the way we came into town." We all looked at the house, and Dad took it. We unloaded the truck and settled in. There was a store right in the fork of the road where we turned off the main road, and we got something to eat. We then made pallets on the floor, and we all slept real good that night.

Chapter 15

Maryland and Mosquitoes

The next morning, Dad was off to go back and get the rest of the family. My brother and I stayed and camped out at the house. We checked everything out, but we mostly rested up. Laying around was very different for us; there was always work to be done, even if only around the house.

The next night we were trying to go to sleep, and we kept hearing sounds like little planes coming in for a landing. Soon after the sounds, we would slap. Something was biting us and hard—it hurt. We finally fell asleep, and morning came. We were scratching on our arms, and little bumps came up. We asked at the store, and the man said it was mosquitoes. I cannot ever remember any mosquitoes in Tennessee. The man at the store said they would not hurt you. This man had an accent, which we later learned was from the Eastern Shore. We had never heard anyone talk like this before, and we thought it was funny talk and enjoyed it. The black man that had given the directions had even more of an accent than the man at the store. When we pulled away from the black man, we were trying to talk like him, and we all laughed a lot about it.

The family showed up, and the house was clean for moving into because my brother and I had been given orders to have the house clean. The windows were clean, the floors were mopped, and everything was in shape. After everyone helped with the unloading of the truck and the beds were set up, they were made up and ready for sleeping. We had every piece in mind, where it was to go and in what room and how to set it up if needed. This made the moving a lot easier and quicker for everyone. We had moved so much that it was like practicing football. Do the practicing enough, and one would learn how to be perfect at it, even moving.

Then off to the new job. I should say, the old job; only the place of work was new. We started out working in the fields right along with the black folks. They were courteous but kept eyeballing trying to figure us out. Are they here to take away our jobs? How long will they stay, and how much of this work do they know? We walked into the field and started working without any teaching. They knew we were not new to the work. They knew that people from Tennessee were coming up every year to do the budding and wrapping of the peach trees. They knew that this work was temporary.

What they did not know was that we were watching them as much as they were watching us. We were working alone, and we finished the row we were on and turned around and came back another row. We finished that row and started the next row. Dad said, "Wait a minute. They are on the first row and only about one fourth the way through the row. We are working too fast." We slowed up and watched and could not believe our eyes that they were that slow at their work. If this was Tennessee, they would be fired; we knew this for a fact. Then Dad said to me, "I'll bet you a quarter if you go over to the fellow that's propped up on the hoe and resting, if you just kick the hoe out from under him it will take him thirty minutes to fall to the ground."

"Why?" I asked.

Dad said, "He is that lazy." We all got the joke and laughed and laughed some more. After I grew up and looked back over my childhood life, I realized that it must take lazy to recognize lazy. Dad was not exactly lazy, but he would never do anything that he could get out of doing.

The black man that gave us the directions was employed at the nursery. His name was Poor Boy, and he was the clown of the place, having fun at whatever he was doing. He was an alcoholic and stayed drunk most of the weekend and drank nightly all week long. His favorite was Sneakie Pete wine, a very cheap wine. Poor Boy was no harm to anyone but himself. He was doing something funny or pulling a joke on someone all the time. The friendship between him and our family was mutual.

Poor Boy got his wine in town on Friday afternoon, and the police saw him. The way Poor Boy walked, one might think he was drunk all the time. The police confronted Poor Boy, and they had words. The police hit Poor Boy in the head with the nightstick. The police took Poor Boy with his head bleeding off to jail. Poor Boy called Mr. Kemp, the owner of the nursery. Mr. Kemp proved that he was not drinking and had been at work all day. Mr. Kemp made them get him a doctor right then to sew up the head, return the wine, and give Poor Boy a ride home with an apology or the town of Prince Ann would be sued.

When it came time for the stitches to come out, Poor Boy would not go to the doctor. Poor Boy said the policeman would still be mad about it, and if the policeman saw him in town, he would take him to jail again. Poor Boy came to my dad and asked, "Will you cut the stitches loose and pull them from my head?"

Dad did so, and the yelling and hollering was unbelievably loud and funny. Dad would fake a stitch pull, and the hollering of "Oh my god" would continue for about a minute. Everyone was watching. His black friends were rolling on the floor and holding their stomachs because of laughing so hard. The teasing began. When they told Poor Boy what was going on, he did not believe them. When he went home that day, Poor Boy got really drunk because he was out of work for two days.

I was in school, and it was really different. The classes were behind in everything, in every subject. Some of the stuff we had already studied. I was in tenth grade and so little that everyone thought I was a freshman. The older kids wanted me to roll up my pant legs, carry their books, and do all kinds of crazy stuff. My friends Fulton and Bruce would tell them to lay off, that I was a sophomore. I was only five foot four, short and little but tough as nails. I went from being a C student to A's and B's on the first report card. Several of the kids wanted to see for themselves that I was making the grades. All the students liked to hear me talk and would gather to hear me tell a story or just answer questions.

We had to ride the bus thirteen miles or more to get to school, and the same on the return trip. This girl had a seat on the bus and a big pile of books next to her. She was sitting upright with good posture and acted like her butt did not stink. I asked her whose books they were, and she shrugged her shoulders, saying "I don't know." I opened the book cover and read the name. "Who is this?" I asked. The girls sitting on the other side of the bus were pointing to the stuck-up. I asked her to pick up her books so I could sit down. She would not. I told her I would put them on the floor if she did not take the books. I did put them on the floor, but she would not sit beside me. She ran up through the bus and wanted to get off. The bus driver would not let her off, and she continued to scream and cry really loud. Then a huge fellow was trying to get in the door of the school bus. He was banging on the door as we were rolling off in the bus. I was sitting in the seat with my face close to the window and was smiling real big as we went by the big fellow. I asked who the big boy was. Everyone said, "Her boyfriend." Then I understood what he was saying: "I'll get you; I am going to whip your butt."

The next day I was waiting on the bus, and here he came. The big boy picked me up by the shoulders of my coat and threw me down the hill about twenty feet. He picked me up again and threw me again. I started trying to get out of the coat so I could move better, but he was on top of me again grabbing at me. I ran backward, and all he got was coat.

This move made him even madder. When he came down the hill, I circled to the up side of the hill. He ran at me, and I ran at him. I jumped in the air and hit him in the mouth with an uppercut. Blood came to his mouth, and he had it on his tongue. With rage in his wild eyes, he came at me again. I was still on the up side of the hill; and when he came again, I ran and jumped in the air, legs open, grabbing him in a scissors hold and grabbing him by the throat at the same time. I tightened my legs up and let all the air go out of him; then I tightened my grip on his throat and would not let go. He beat me in the back and in the back of my head, but I would not loosen my grip. He began to stumble and get weak. Without air coming in, he was weak and fell to the ground. While he was falling to the ground, I undid the scissors hold to free my legs and we hit the ground together. I began bouncing his head off the ground and back to the ground.

When the kids said, "Stop, he's turning blue, you are going to kill him," I turned him loose. I shook my finger at him, telling him if he wanted some more to come back tomorrow. I caught the bus and went home; I did not have a problem getting a seat. The next day a bigger boy showed up looking for me. The bigger boy looked down at me after someone pointed me out to him and said, "You are the one that whipped Charlie." I told him yes. Fulton and Bruce wanted to get in on the fighting, and they were saying, "It's my turn, no, it's my turn." The big boy was not looking at them but was looking at me, and he starting laughing. He was saying as he walked away, "Charlie needed his butt kicked if he could not whip such a little boy." Charlie was six foot two inches tall and looked like a giant to me.

The word got out, and everyone was calling me "Little Tennessee." I would be walking down the hallway; the students would point and say, "That's Little Tennessee." Some would laugh and ask, "Are you sure?" I was proud of myself.

That summer Charlie was selling watermelons on the square of Princess Ann. I walked over and said hey to him. He spoke back and turned a little red in the face, but never got up from where he was sitting.

My dad, brother, and I had been working at night at the nursery. Three nights, four hours a night. We were packing and wrapping trees, grading and bundling the trees, and getting them ready for shipping. This is called working in the packinghouse. With winter over and all the main shipping done, the night shift was over until the next year.

School would be out soon, and back in the fields we would go. We would work in the fields until June budding season started. Then all of us would work in the June budding all summer long. From June budding we would move to dorm budding and all the other buddings of trees. Our younger brother would be working again this year with all of us.

Yes, the dog made the trip okay. We were upstairs, and he started barking. We went to the window to see what he was barking at. It was a deer at the edge of the woods behind the house. This was the first deer that any of us had seen. Mac ran across the field and was trying to catch the deer. The deer jumped twice and ran into the woods. When he blew at the dog, Mac stopped in surprise and turned and came back to the house. We all talked about the deer: how pretty it was and how fast it was.

Chapter 16

Strawberry Farm

We moved again, this time farther out, about eight miles. The place belonged to the nursery. Dad had to do upkeep work and watch the farm but paid very little in rent for us to live there. The river was not far from the house. It joined the back side of the farm along one field. The river had a tide just like the oceans. The river was called Wicomico, and it ran into the Chesapeake Bay, which had a tide. The farm was neat and had plenty of buildings on it. It had a barn, a toolshed or barn, and a strawberry barn that was turned into an asparagus bundling house. This was a good place to play during the winter months or when it was raining. We mostly shot marbles or played various games with the marbles.

The house was big and roomy. Going into the front door, the room on the left was Dad and Mom's room. The room to the right was the living room. The stairs were in front of you inside the front door. Upstairs, the room to the left was Uncle Robert's and straight ahead was our room for the boys and to the right was a room for the other boys. Downstairs, down the hallway past Dad's room was the girls' room on the left. The house had a front porch and a back porch that was screened in. The kitchen was big and had plenty of room for a table, chairs, and a long wooden bench for us six kids. The house had vents in the floor where the heat could rise up and heat the upstairs. This was the first heat that we had ever had upstairs.

We worked all summer long every day that we were not rained out, and we were making good money. This nursery paid better than the nurseries in Tennessee. We were liking it just fine up here in Maryland. We were starting to buy better clothes and better things and getting a taste of the good life. We were taking on a new look, which was an improvement for all of us. We boys had never seen our checks, and now we got an allowance. Our oldest brother was still our personal driver when we went to town for a movie. I was learning how to drive and doing okay, but I only drove on the back roads.

We went to the river and swam on Saturday or Sunday. My friend Fulton lived about two miles down the road. He lived in a large family too. He drove and brought his sisters and brothers to the river for a swim too. When all of us were down at the river, it made for a really big fun time. All of the kids up and down the road rode the school bus together and were close friends.

With summer about gone, school would be starting soon and then there would be homework every afternoon as soon as I got home. We still had chores to do and still took turns doing the dishes. We also had to split the kindling to start fires and carry up the firewood and the wood for the kitchen stove.

I got interested in sports a little bit. I watched football, baseball, boxing, and wrestling. We did not have a TV yet; the radio was our link to the outside world. We started watching TV at Dad's cousin's apartment at the nursery. We would get off work late at night and go watch boxing on Friday nights. Sometimes we watched wrestling, and it was fun and entertaining to us. We tried some of the holds and made believe that we were professionals. I found out that I could not stand to be on the bottom of the pile; when someone hollered pile on, they all piled on me. For some reason I would go bananas and had to come out from under the pile. It was like I was losing my breath.

I found out another thing about myself. The house had a little leak that was running down in the kitchen. The nursery owner called the roofer to come out and make repairs.

The roofer had ladders everywhere. One led up on the porch roof, another one ran from the porch roof to the roof over the kitchen, and another one reached to the high part of the house that was the attic over the bedrooms. I had never climbed that high outside in the open before. I had climbed the bales of hay in the barn, which was higher than the rooftop. We boys would take a rope and swing out high off the high part of the bales of hay and free-fall into a big pile of hay that was in the loft of the big, big barn on the Burton farm.

I started to climb the ladder, and the roofer told me not to go up there. I climbed to the porch roof anyway and stood there, and the roofer and I talked. He said, "The roof is higher than you think. Have you ever been on top of a house before?"

I said, "No, but I have been high in the barn before."

He said, "There is a big difference when you are outside under the open sky."

I stood around a little while, and on up the next ladder I went. I looked around and down, and it felt good. The roofer was busy doing something to the roof and did not see me climb the last ladder; I was right beside him when he turned his head and saw me. I moved around up on the roof, looking out over the fields and down the road. It was beautiful, I thought. Then I started down and moved toward the ladder. Looking down where I had to go, I froze up. I could not move; I just sat there. I called out to the roofer and said I couldn't move.

The roofer said, "This happens all the time on the first climb." He told me to sit still—like I wasn't already still; hell, I could not move. The roofer told me to relax and think about something that I really liked. He suggested swimming, hunting, fishing. I said fishing. I started thinking about fishing because I was learning how to use Dad's 202 Zebco reel. The roofer told me when I felt comfortable, to hold on the ladder with one hand, put the palm of my other hand down on the roof, and swing my leg over the top of the ladder and put my foot on the top step of the ladder. "Push off the roof with the palm hand and hold onto the other side of the ladder and be still for a moment and keep looking at me. Do not look at the ground."

I did exactly what he said, and down I went to the next level and to the next level and then I was on the ground. My legs were weak and trembling, and it took several minutes to get myself back together. I said I was sorry about it. The roofer was real nice, and he said there was no need for an apology. To this day, I still can't climb unless I have something to hold onto.

Sometimes I think finding out about yourself is the biggest part about growing up. One has to know their limits. How fast can you run, and how long can you run? Are you afraid of heights, and are you afraid of water? Can you fight without getting mad? Can you lose and be a good sport about it? Is winning at any cost everything to you? *All* these things need to be answered before you grow up and accept responsibility of any kind, especially a family.

We were back in school, and I was doing okay for a country boy from Tennessee. We had changed schools and gone on up the road to the big high school this year. I continued to make good grades, and for some reason everyone was real nice to me. I really did not know how to feel; I really didn't. There is always someone trying to pick on little people or make fun of them. Here I could hold my head up high and walk down the hallways and feel just as important as everyone else—and I was.

There was a first-aid class in biology, and I liked it very much. It taught me how to apply a tourniquet and how to clean and take care of a cut so that it would not get infected. It taught us everything that was known about first aid in those days. We also got into tree planting. This I knew how to do. When the trees showed up and we went outside to plant the trees, I took over. When the students started to do something wrong, I said, "Can I show you how to do it so you won't kill the tree?" My teacher was all smiles and liked the help that she was getting.

Mom and Dad went to Tennessee on a short vacation and to pick up our grandpa. They brought Grandpa back to stay awhile with us. Dad had only one car, and we boys had to have transportation. The nursery loaned us a truck to go back and forth to work. My older brother had his driver's license now. My next-younger brother and I wanted to ride in the back of the big truck. There were tools laying all over in the back of the truck. We all wanted to go get some things at the store, about three miles up the road. We were ready to go back home and had our candy, soft drink or soda pop, and whatever, and we were eating the stuff. Then a car pulled out in front of us, and my brother had to put on his brakes real fast.

My younger brother went sliding along the truck bed and slid into the briar blade handfirst. This briar blade has a blade three feet long and very sharp for cutting blackberry briars. It cut my brother's fingers, one of them almost off. I saw what had happened and screamed out to my brother, telling him to go to the hospital and make it quick. I got my brother to sit down; and holding on with the other hand, I grabbed hold of his wrist, gripped real tight, and stopped the bleeding. I was making a tourniquet with my hands. There was not anything to make one out of, and this was the next best thing. I released my grip every seven to ten minutes to get blood in the hand again. The blood would puddle up in the palm, and I would turn over his hand and pour out the blood while talking to my brother. There was not very much pain, and he had stopped crying and we were making jokes about it.

We got him to the doctor and got him sewed up. The doctor said he was going to be all right. He had to sew a ligament back together. The doctor asked what we did to help him on the way there. I told him about the makeshift tourniquet with my hands, applying pressure and then letting it off. The doctor said I did good and did the right thing.

The ride home was good and relaxing because my older brother and I had done good under pressure once again. I thought, *school is not too bad after all*. I was glad the biology course was available for me and the other kids. One never knows when your knowledge will be used to help someone or help yourself.

Spring was coming, and this meant that school would be letting out soon. I had started reading again and was reading books on the Black Stallion; the Black Stallion's son and his offspring; and Bonfire, a harness racer. On warm days after I had my chores done, I grabbed a book and went off to my secret hiding place to read. The reason I would hide was that too many people, especially Mom, could always find something for me to do. The winters were not as cold as back in Tennessee. I would put my coat on and slip out of the house and around the house on the sunny side where the chimney was. I would sit with my back to the wall and the chimney, and this served as a wind blocker for me. Sometimes I would have to change sides because of the wind direction. I read every chance I could get. I also learned every joke I heard at school, and there were plenty of them. I got so good at remembering jokes that after hearing them just one time, the joke was in my memory.

We boys went fishing with Uncle Robert. We caught an eel and we ran away, not knowing what it was. Uncle Robert got it off the hook, but he had a time doing it. Then we caught a turtle—a big turtle. We caught a few fish, and then to the house we went. We cleaned the turtle. It had twenty-eight eggs in it. Turtles are good to eat and healthy for you. I've been told there are about five or more different tastes in the meat. There are beef, pig, chicken, rabbit, goat, and sheep tastes all in the turtle.

I was trying to figure out what I was going to do with the turtle eggs. I hated to see them go to waste. The eggs are tough, and you can throw them and they will not bust very easily. The eggs have to be thrown very hard against a wall in order to bust them. We have played with the eggs, throwing them and hitting each other with them. They soften up a little but are still tough.

Come Monday I loaded up my pockets with the eggs, and off to school I went. While riding the bus, we picked up Fulton and then Bruce, and I showed the eggs to them in that order. We decided not to tell anyone about the eggs. I gave each one of them five eggs, and I had plenty left. Fulton and Bruce both said I was going to knock some heads with them. I told them that throwing them against someone's head would not bust them. They did not believe me. We got to school, and they threw their eggs as hard as they could and hit students in the back, but the eggs did not break. We went on to class; and when that class was over, they tried it again, with the same results. They could not get the eggs back, because they were being kicked around on the floor.

About that time a girl screamed out and started jumping up and down. She dropped her book and was standing bent over at the waist, holding onto her skirt and looking at her legs. She ran screaming to the bathroom. We boys started laughing because we had figured out what had happened. The girls wore skirts with the little poodle dogs on them and ruffles under the skirts. They wore two-tone shoes of black and white, and rock and roll was on the rise. This girl was walking down the hall and had stepped on the egg with the hard-sole shoes and an egg busted, sending egg spraying up her legs. Since the yoke had broken, the spray was yellow; this scared the crap out of her. I, Bruce, and Fulton were still laughing and went on to the next class. We knew what we were going to do with the rest of the eggs.

When we came out of class, we each threw three eggs in the busy hallway and stood back and watched. The same thing happened all over again. All of us were standing in the locker area and laughing our butts off. We were seeing the legs high up on some of the girls. The boys were mad and cussing and took their handkerchiefs and tried to wipe the egg yellow off, but they were spreading it more than anything. The boys dressed in khaki pants with the legs rolled up to show their socks and two-tone shoes, with their hair combed real neat and wildroot cream oil on their hair. We finally figured out why the best-dressed got the egg treatment. They were more of them, and they all had hard-sole shoes on. This would bust the egg and let it spray out. As the egg was stepped on, the egg would roll over a little and the edge would be between the hard floor and the hard shoe sole; this would point the spray upward. Word got out that some of the yellow got on panties.

Then the intercom came on, and the principal said that anyone caught with eggs would be suspended for the rest of the year. Well, I had about five or six left in my locker. Bruce, Fulton, and I talked it over. I knew what I had to do: get the eggs and flush them down the commode. I did it. On the way home on the school bus, I asked, "How did he know what the yellow stuff was? Did he taste it?" We all laughed, and it was a big day with lots of fun.

I was learning how to drive in driver's ed, and it was a lot of fun. I already knew how to drive. What I needed was practice and more practice. I never carried the book home with me because I did not have one. I would borrow a book and do the homework that day and return the book. I made 100 percent on the written test, and the students could not understand how I did it. The teacher made a big deal about it bragging on me.

I also took typing that year, and I shouldn't have. I had booked myself with six subjects. After I learned the keyboard and was typing about forty words a minute, I thought that was all I needed. I explained to the teacher that she would have to give me a failing grade because I did not have time to study the rest of the subjects and do all my homework at home because I had to work at night; I needed the typing class time as a study hall. The teacher said she would check and maybe I could be transferred to a study hall class, but that did not work. The teacher said, "As long as you study and do not interfere with the rest of the class, you can study in the back of this room. It's okay with me." So she gave me a special seat at the back of the room, and I studied and got my homework done. I'm glad I learned typing; it's coming in handy now.

The night work started, and we worked four nights a week. We worked Monday, Tuesday, Thursday, and Friday; we had Wednesday off in the middle of the week to rest a little so that it would not be so hard on us. One night all of us were grading and bundling trees and filling orders, with a joke here and there. I said I knew a lot of dirty jokes. All of the men urged me to start telling the jokes. They made a seat for me, and everyone moved their work as close as they could so I would not have to talk so loud. I asked my dad if I could tell the jokes using the dirty words like I heard them. We were poor, but Dad did not allow us kids to cuss or smoke. He said, "Tell your jokes, but you can't tell them around the house or use the bad words around the house." Dad thought I knew only about six or eight jokes. The old man was surprised, and I think he was a little proud too. I told jokes for about two hours.

I never told the same joke twice unless I was asked to repeat the joke so they could figure it out and remember it. Both the blacks and the whites were laughing hard and having fun. When I started telling the jokes, I told the blacks that they were black jokes too. They said, "Let her rip," and I did.

The junior boss came back there and saw me one night while I was telling the jokes. His name was Richard, and he was very young to be in charge. He was mad and told me to get back to work and that if I told another joke he would fire me. Well, here came the other boss. He grabbed Richard by the arm and led him off and up into the packing shed, where he chewed his butt out and sent him home. He then came back to where we were and told us to go on with whatever we were doing. One of the black men asked, "Mr. Kemp, can he still tell the jokes?" Mr. Kemp replied, "Yes, he can, as long as the work continues at the same pace as it is now." So the joke telling went on.

The next night, all the grown-ups, both blacks and whites, were talking. One of the black men said he heard Mr. Kemp chewing out Richard, the young boss. The black man said Mr. Kemp said that the packinghouse was getting out more work now than before and Richard should get his butt to the house and stay there. We all laughed about it. The same man continued, "I knew we were doing a good job." Everyone agreed with him, and the work continued on.

The nursery had an old black man working there, and I mean real old. They all said that Charlie started to work there when he was a young boy. Everyone called him Uncle Charlie out of respect, and we did too. His sidekick was named Nolen; and everywhere you saw Charlie, you would see Nolen. They had a house they rented together. Uncle Charlie smoked cigars, and they had a good smell. Uncle Charlie would cut them into halves before he would smoke one of them. Everyone liked Uncle Charlie without doubt. He would smoke the cigar half, smoke it all the way to his lips; the ashes would fall from his lips, and he would not waste a bit of the cigar. Uncle Charlie did this time after time and never burned his lips. Everyone told the story that Mr. Kemp, the founder of the nursery, left it in his will that Uncle Charlie had a job as long as he could make it into work, so long as he did not steal anything and came in to work sober.

Just about everybody at the nursery had a nickname. I was called Cotton Top; and there were Egghead, Peckerhead, Poor Boy, P, Little Richard, Big Richard, Peck—I think this was short for henpecked, Sput, Mugs, Spuds, and on and on. This was my dad's doing; whoever did not have a nickname was going to get one whether he wanted one or not. All my dad had to do was call someone a name in a conversation and start joking about it, and it would stick. Everyone would start using the nickname. Like that would make you an egghead, right?

Chapter 17

The Wristwatch

Summer was almost upon us again. School was behind us for another year, and the long hot days in the fields were beginning. I had been looking at a watch at the store where the school bus would let the schoolkids off the bus to go on up the road. The bus would stop and pick us up on the way back through. The watch was a fine-looking watch for the wrist. I knew I would look good in this wristwatch. I started saving up the money for the watch, called a Timex. They cost about fifteen dollars, and I had almost fourteen dollars saved up already. I wanted to get the watch, but I did not want to be broke after I bought it. The wristwatch would have to wait awhile longer.

My older brother told my dad that he needed to do what he wanted to do with his money now. My dad made a deal with him to pay so much a week while he was still living there. My brother had worked ever since he was big enough. He helped in keeping the family from starving to death and gave all his money to Mom and Dad without ever complaining and asking for much. This was the thanks for it: a deal to pay board at his own home. My brother helped more to make it a home than my dad or my mom. I include my mom in it because she could have put a stop to it at anytime, but she did not.

My brother changed his appearance by buying his clothes and shopping for himself, buying what he wanted to wear instead of Mom doing the shopping. I was happy and excited about the new car that he bought. It was a 1956 two-door Ford Fairlane, desert rose in color, and beautiful. He had two glass-packed mufflers put on it, and did it sound good! When it got warmed up and the mufflers got burned out, what a sound. Everyone in the town of Princess Ann knew whose car it was. There was no other color like this color around anywhere. It outran everything in town. Several times he raced Chevrolets after the owners bought something else to make them faster. Some of them would beat him on the drag, but on the top end they never had a chance. The Chevrolets blew up and their transmissions failed, but the Ford was still running. While turning a curve, my brother bent the frame. It got out of alignment and would wear out a set of tires pronto. It would cost about eight hundred dollars to correct the problem, so he traded the Ford off. Six years later, he saw the Ford still running, and it did not smoke a bit. He was happy to talk to the owner about it. The owner said, "It's fast and I don't know how fast. I'm not going to find out either."

The summer work was going just fine, and everyone was having fun while working hard. We would work all week, nine and a half hours a day. When Saturday came, we got the energy to go swimming. After swimming, we would come home and get ready to go to town to see the movies. The westerns were our favorites, and we looked forward to it each week. My older brother would drop us off at the movies, and he would go to the ballpark and watch the games, talk about car racing, or whatever. But always when it came time to pick us up at the movies, he was there. There was only one time I can remember him being late, and that was about forty-five minutes. When I asked, "Where were you? What took so long?" my brother said, "I don't want to talk about it." We did not talk about it, and I never asked again.

During the summer, when we boys worked full-time, our allowance—or payoff money—was a little more than in the winter months. I would have money for the movies and could save a little money toward the wristwatch.

Around midsummer Dad and Mom were talking loud on purpose. I could hear it along with everyone else. They were talking about money that had to be paid on a bill. They had already asked Uncle Robert for the money, and he said he did not have any money. They asked me, and I said I didn't have the money.

Mom said, "What about the money you have hidden in your room?"

Mom must have searched my room and found the money. I thought I had hidden it real good. I said, "That money is for the watch that I'm going to buy."

Dad asked for the money, and I told him no. Dad grabbed me by the throat, and I grabbed him on each wrist with each hand. He picked me up and slammed me against the wall. After three or four slams against the wall, he stopped and let me slip down to my feet, with my throat still in his hand a little bit. I got my breath back and said, "You might as well kill me 'cause I'm not giving you the money. If you want the money, go steal it from me."

Dad finally released me from his grip and let me go. Dad said, "I only wanted to borrow the damn money."

I said, "When you borrow from us, you don't ever pay back." I knew he had borrowed money from Uncle Robert and Grandpa and never paid it back.

Talking to my brother recently about some of this stuff, I found out that Dad left Tennessee on the run. My brother said he had six or seven outstanding loans and that the bank and the loan companies had found him through school records and run him down. My brother said he mortgaged the old mules over and over again, and he had sold them about three years ago. I remember

Mom telling Dad that a man came out to the house one day that week, but I did not know what about. My brother said that it was the loan people telling him to pay up or go to jail; Dad had falsified the bank records by putting down the mules for the loans not once but several times, and this was a crime.

I don't know where the money came from to send to the bank. Dad did not go to jail, and he did not get my wristwatch money. This was the last of the loans to be paid back. My brother said we had paid off all of them in about two years.

The watch sure did look good on my wrist, and I was the only one that knew how much trouble I had getting it. I had to save the money up over a long period of time. Then there was the trouble of not giving up the money to my mom and dad. My mom would do anything for my dad, even if it meant that her children would have to be sacrificed of their possessions and punished for their conveniences.

When my brother got his freedom and broke away on his own, he was a little over seventeen; this gave me something to look forward to. It also gave me courage to stand up to my parents. Looking back and thinking about it all gives me another view of what happened back then. I think my brother and I were growing up and were going to jump out of the nest. Dad was thinking, *I'm losing my free labor, and what am I going to do?* Well, things started to change little by little for us older kids. Dad knew that one of us had flown the coop and another in one year was going to fly off too. Then another in two years, and this meant that three out of six would be gone. But he still had three left, and just maybe my baby sister will write about it. I was working all the time and in school. There was very little time that was spent with the younger siblings. I was busy from a very young age and hired out at ten and a half years old, and my older brother was in the same fix. So we did not have any growing-up pains; we grew up so fast time just passed us by. Sometimes I think it made me stronger—hell, I know it did. My little sister told me that when she got up, I had already left the house, and when I came in she was already in bed. That's when I was in high school and working nights and all summer long.

Summer was finally almost gone and I would be back in school. I could rest up after working all summer long in the hot fields. Then I would have to get ready for the packinghouse and the night work. Being young let me regain my strength very quickly and be ready for the next task.

I found out I could do mechanic work if I had to. Dad had a 1949 Plymouth; it was a fine-driving car, and I liked it. I was learning to drive, and this car was taking me to the store and swimming and wherever on the back roads. This being a very sandy state was a problem for the '49 Plymouth. It had a band around the starter where the bushings are to keep out foreign debris. But the sand kept getting into the starter and locking it up. I had to take off the starter and clean it every so often and put it back on if I wanted to drive the car. My dad told me what to do and went back in the house, and I had to fix it or stay at home. The first time, I worked about three hours and was worn out. I cleaned up and stayed home. Each time got easier and faster. I put the tools in the car just in case it needed work on the road.

Mom and Dad made a trip back to Tennessee for a visit, so they said, and a vacation, all in one. We boys had to fend for ourselves, and it was not hard to do with the upbringing we had. We could cook, wash dishes, do the clothes-washing, or whatever came up. Mom and Dad were not worried at all, nor did they care.

A month had gone by since Dad and Mom returned from the trip. I had already started school along with the rest of us kids. I was settled in the eleventh grade and doing just fine. My favorite class this year was biology, and I was enjoying it to the fullest. I got good grades in every subject except English, and even there I got a C. I got the first six-week report card, and I was looking good. Three weeks later, Dad told us we were moving back to Tennessee.

They had been waiting on a house to open up, but had not said a word to any of us. Mom got a letter in the mail and had to go to a pay telephone to call and say they would take the apartment.

My older brother, who had a girlfriend and a job, told Dad and Mom that he was not going. I did not like this part of it. But after thinking about it, I realized that he would be better off on his own. I knew he was tough enough to make it and he would not have any trouble. This meant the oldest had flown the nest, and the rest were yet to go. My older brother grew up faster than any kid that I ever knew. He was acting like an adult at the age of ten. In fact, he was more grown-up than my mom or my dad. We kids did not cuss or swear or smoke or drink. Dad always said, "If you're going to drink or smoke or chew or dip, you have to buy your own." Dad took all of our money, so this eliminated the problem—and I think he knew it. I never wanted to do any of those things, so it did not bother me. We were taught not to steal; "If you want something, work for it." My older brother knew responsibility and that the young came first. One needed to protect the family, take care of the younger siblings. He knew the management of money, where to spend and not to spend, and when to spend. It was like going from knee britches to being an adult overnight. I did not know this at the time or ever put much thought into it until I started comparing things from my memory and talking to other kids. I often have thought since of this: if he had not grown up so fast and taken responsibility on himself, what would have happened to the family?

We were loaded up and going to leave. The sad part was we were leaving our brother behind. We had never been separated like this before, but I had all the confidence in the world that he would be all right and make it on his own.

Chapter 18

Dossett Homes

We got moved in and settled in the new neighborhood. We had to learn our way around. This area was new to all of us kids. Grandma had the apartment three doors up and on the right in the next row of houses. Over in the back of the apartment across the backyard was another friend of my mom's, Mrs. Foster. She was friends of the family when we lived on Maplewood Avenue. So this was like homecoming for my mom. I was sure glad to see Grandma and gave her a big hug. She said I had grown a lot, but I knew she was just trying to make me feel good. I did not remember much about Mrs. Foster from when we lived on Maplewood Avenue. I knew her, but there was not a personal connection. I started to know Mrs. Foster and her children as time went by. Mrs. Foster had lost her husband and so was qualified for the apartment. Her husband had been in the military, but died from natural causes.

I started to the new school and was getting caught up on everything. Maryland had been behind in everything, and I had to catch up and fast. I started shop class this year and liked it. I made a few friends, but most of the students were heads-up-in-the-air types. The government had put the Arnold Engineering Development Center just outside of Tullahoma. The wages out there were the best in the state. It did not take long for the kids to feel rich because they had cars, good clothes, and money to spend on whatever. This made them stuck-up. This did not bother me, but I remember it.

In English class I was having a tough time of it. For some reason the teacher did not like me; to this day I have not figured out why. This teacher liked for people to recite poems and Shakespeare. Since my last name started with the letter C, I was always to start first no matter what. I had to break the ice on every recital, and this set the tone every time. I did not have time to look at the poem and read it over to have it in my mind before she wanted me to stand up and start reciting. This was before roll call because this was how she checked the roll.

One day I knew the poem really well and had been practicing all day. When I got into class, she called on me to say my poem. I stood up and informed her I would not go first today. Then I sat back down. The teacher asked a second time, and I repeated that I would not go first. The teacher asked why, and I told her that it was not fair for me to break the ice every time. She told me to go first or I would have to go to the office and get a paddling for not doing what she said. I got up and said, "Let's go to the office and get the paddling." We did. When we came back to the classroom and she asked again, I again said no. I got up from my desk and started for the door. At the office I got another paddling. I returned to the classroom, and she asked again. I got up and headed for the office and got another paddling.

The principal asked me why I would not say the poem. I explained that I had to go first every time and that the teacher was picking on me. The principal asked, "Do you know the poem?" I said yes, and the principal told me to recite it. I gathered my thoughts and started saying the poem. Then the principal said, "That's enough. You go stand in the hallway and send the teacher back in here." He asked the teacher all kinds of questions and chewed her butt out real good, and she came out of the office crying.

I must admit I had tears in my eyes on the last paddling. That was three bustings of the butt in a row. The teacher told me to stay after class, and I did. When all the kids had left the classroom, she apologized to me and said if I came back this afternoon after school, she would let me say the poem and make the grade up. I did just that and got a B+. After that, we got along just fine, and my grades got a lot better.

I was good in Algebra 1, and I made almost straight As. This teacher we'll call Mr. H, and I will get back to him at a later time. He was my history teacher in the twelfth grade, so we won't lose him or forget.

I was very good in shop class because I was very good with my hands and did not mind the work. I made lamps, checkerboards, small end tables, and everything I could get to and have time to finish before school was out for the summer. I really enjoyed making things out of wood.

Gym class was one of those classes that did not go so well this year. The coach had us split up into teams and play basketball. I could get up and down the court and run the whole time without getting winded. This gave me the advantage; when they got tired, I was just warming up. We could not call time-outs; the only time there was any rest was when the coach called a foul and the game slowed up for the free throws. Under the basket, the taller boys would out-rebound me, because I was five foot five and the shortest kid in the junior class.

There was a boy about six feet tall who kept jumping up for the rebound and throwing his butt in my face. He would grab the ball and at the same time throw his butt out so no one could defend against it. He was laughing when we went back down the floor. I told him that twice was enough of the showing off, and the next time he threw his butt in my face that he would be picking it up off the floor. He laughed real big and down the court we went. His team scored, and back up the court we went. One of our players shot and missed, and the tall boy was in position for the rebound. He went up for the rebound, and out came his butt in my face; I grabbed him by the waist, and he went to the floor in a floor slam. A fight broke out; they were going to fight me, and I was ready. The biggest player on the other team stepped out to fight me, and the biggest boy on our team stepped in between and told him he was not going to do anything. The boy raised his fist, and my teammate knocked him out and two of the players were on the floor. By this time the coach was on top of the situation, blowing the whistle fast and hard. The coach said, "No fighting," brought on two more teams, and told us to sit down on the bleachers and wait for him.

The coach asked what the fight was about; because he was looking straight at me, I said, "It was just a misunderstanding." The other boys were walking by and saying, "We are going to get you." The coach told everyone to go get showered and he would finish checking it out the next day. Everyone was off to the showers, and down the steps I went. Three boys were waiting for me; they started punching me, and we were fighting. I hit one in the jaw and knocked him backward. The boy that had been bottom slammed I had by the throat with one hand; I hit him in the face and kicked the other boys with my foot to keep them off me. I came out with a few knots and a bloody lip. The bottom-slammed boy had two black eyes; the second boy had one black eye, and the third boy walked around like he had a broken rib. I was not in a fight after that for the rest of the year or the next.

These boys decided fighting me was not a good idea. They were planning their revenge, however, and I was going to be ready for it. I had finished playing a scrimmage game of basketball. The coach told all of us to sit and watch the other scrimmage games. I was sweating profusely, and the sweat had made my T-shirt wet. Suddenly, my back was on fire; it was burning. But I could not figure out why. I stood up and pulled my T-shirt off. I could not see anything on the T-shirt, so I put it back on. My back began burning again. I pulled my T-shirt off again. This time I smelled something when the T-shirt went over my head. It was a bad smell, and my eyes started burning. I went and told the coach that I was going to the showers. I showed my back to the coach, and it was red and burning. I took a long shower and used the soap to bring relief. I came back to sit down but immediately turned and ran back to the showers. Class had let out, and everyone was in the showers now. I stepped out and dried off, and the burning started again. I stepped back in the showers and stayed there for a good twenty minutes. My eyes had stopped burning during the first shower. It was nothing compared to the skunk spraying me.

The coach came by and asked for my T-shirt as I was drying off. The next day the coach told me that the chemical on my T-shirt was mustard gas. The coach said whoever did it must have gotten it from the chemistry lab. The coach set all of us boys down and said that anyone caught with the mustard gas would be expelled permanently from the school and would not graduate. I never did find out who did this to me. Their lips were sealed because they knew I would retaliate. I did find out how they got the mustard gas on me without me knowing it; they had used a water pistol.

That was the most shower-taking that I had ever done in one day. My hands were the cleanest ever. There is another story about clean hands that I will tell you later.

I heard one of the kids talking about working for the bowling alley. Being in the job hunt, I started asking questions about the money and what you had to do for the money. He said, "You have to set pins all night long."

I said, "All night long?"

He laughed and said, "Through the week is league nights, and when the league is over you can go home."

"What is setting pins?"

"They knock them down and we set them back up so they can knock them down again."

"Are they hiring now?"

"Yes."

"Can I go with you tonight and find out where and who to see?"

"Yes, you can."

I met him at the grocery store, and we walked across town to the bowling alley. I got a job and started that night. I learned how to set pins real fast, and after one week I was ready for the league bowling. This was where the money was at. The more I could make, the better off I was. I was going to pay for schooling and school lunches. Then I would buy my school clothes. I would work here all winter; and when school was out, I would go to work at the nursery again. When summer was over, I would go back to the bowling alley for the winter months. Then school would be out, and I would be graduating. Then I would go look for the big job.

When the school year ended, I had passed everything, and this pleased me. I had to start thinking how I was going to get to work at the nursery. I found out that a truck came to town every morning and made pickups and dropped off in the afternoons. There were no fees for this, which made me happy. I went over to the meeting point, climbed on the truck, and went to the nursery. I got a job by just saying who I was. I worked there all summer long and saved up my money. I did not stash it in my room. I got Charlie's grandma's son to hide it in his room and not tell anyone about it. If Mom and Dad knew, they would be trying to borrow it or talk me out of it. I acted broke all the time. I worked all summer long at the nursery.

I came home after a nine-and-a-half-hour day and was dirty all over. I had only one thing on my mind—a bath and clean clothes. Some of the neighborhood kids stopped me—two boys and a girl—and wanted to borrow some money. I asked, "How are you going to pay it back? You don't work anywhere, so where is the money coming from to pay me back?"

They said, "We'll pay you back. Just lend us the money. We want to go skating tonight because it's a special night at the skating rink."

I pulled out five dollars from my wallet and put the wallet back. Their eyes were real big, and I could tell they thought I was going to lend them the money. I bent over and laid the five dollars on the sidewalk and said, "There are three of you and one of me. If you three can get to the money and get it, you can have it."

Their eyes got bigger yet, and they started looking at one another and moving in and out. The biggest boy lowered his shoulder, and here he came; I popped his head and let him go by. The other boy was working with the girl; he was to draw me toward him, and she would run in and pick up the money. When she ran in, she was bent forward at the waist a little; I kicked her in the chest just above the milk factory. It flipped her, and she landed on the sidewalk and started crawling backward away from me. She started crying, and the boys were saying, "My older brother will be seeing you. You're crazy." They walked away.

I hollered, "Come and get the money. Tell your brother I walk this way home every day after work." They were lazy kids and wanted something for nothing, and it never happened.

The dog Mac made the trip back to Tennessee with us, and he was okay. A hurricane came through Maryland, and it had all of us scared. The big farmhouse raised up, shook, and almost left the foundation but settled back down. This scared the dog so much that he jumped up in my dad's lap. A tree blew through the roof and part of the screen on the back porch. My older brother and the brother just younger than I went in the truck down the road to our neighbor's house to see if he was okay. Mr. Townsen was an old man and lived by himself; it was just him and the dog named Jack. When my brothers got there, Mr. Townsen was on the ground and the wind was blowing so hard he could not make it back to the house. Mr. Townsen had gone out to close up the chicken houses just before dark. My brothers helped him back into the house, and he was okay. Then they went back outside to close up the chicken houses. A board hit my brother in the forehead, but he did not think much of it.

The next day all of us went by to check on Mr. Townsen, and we were looking around to see if everything was okay. On the corner of the chicken house where my brother had been hit was a two-by-four with a nail in the end of it. We have no way of knowing if it was the same board that hit him in the forehead. We were thinking about the nail and how lucky my brother was and thinking the Lord was taking care of him. The wind was blowing in gusts up to 115 miles per hour. This was our first hurricane, and I hope we don't have to go through another one.

Our town was growing by leaps and bounds, and the new high school was catching everyone's eyes when we drove by the summer before it was completed. This was a million-dollar high school, and we were to be the first seniors in the new school. I started back to school in the fall, and the new school took some getting used to. Finding our way around and where everything was took about a week of looking; then the new started wearing off, and we settled in for the year.

I was talking to one of my friends, and the class ring came up. I asked how much the ring cost. My friend said it had been 210 dollars the previous year. I said I was already saving money, and I would be ready. My friend had a paper route, but he said, "I'll have a rough time saving that much money up."

I was back at the bowling alley four nights a week and going to school full-time. My friend would come by and pick me up, and we rode to school together. I paid him for the gas, and I helped him sling papers on the weekends when we were double-dating. One weekend we had our dates and were riding around and I was driving his car. I had my license now and was legal to drive. My friend was drinking another beer after the first one tasted so good to him. He started acting out like he was drunk, and his girlfriend was holding onto him by the belt as he hung out the window. He was screaming and yelling and making the girls scream and yell too. We were on a city street, and I was driving along very slow.

I asked his girlfriend if she was getting tired holding onto him. She said yes. I told my friend to pull himself back in the car and settle down, but he would not. I asked several times, but he would not. I told his girlfriend to let me have the belt and I would hold onto him for a while. She did, and was working the feeling back in her arms. I asked my friend again to get back in the car. When he refused again, I dumped him in the street headfirst at about fifteen miles per hour. There was a big yell outside the car; inside it was quiet, and both girls were holding their breath and could not speak. I got out after stopping and asked my friend, "Are you okay?"

He said, "Are you trying to kill me?"

I said, "No, I'm trying to get you to be quiet and quit worrying the girls. If I was trying to kill you, I would have speeded up to about sixty and dumped you out." I had no trouble out of my friend after that. Whenever I told him to stop doing something, he stopped.

My friend had a bump on his head, a skinned place on his forehead at the hairline, and a little skin off one of his hands. He was willing to suffer that for the attention that he was getting and the attention that was yet to come. They got married two years later.

The shop work was coming along. I still made everything as good and as fast as I could. I was filling up the house with things I made. I was doing okay in the other subjects too. My friend and I were getting to school early, waiting on the milkman and helping him unload. He gave us milk to drink for the labor because most of the time we had not eaten a regular breakfast. I would grab a biscuit going out the door, and my friend would get something on the move too as he was running the paper route.

We had another friend and hung with him in school and had classes with him. All of our last names started with the letter C. We call ourselves the Three C's. With about three months left in the school year, the history teacher I told you about earlier, Mr. H, was up to some old tricks and we had to catch him. When you went into the classroom, my row of seats was next to the windows. We got to thinking about it one day and talking to one another. The three C's were fact-finding. Every one of us in the window row was having to work our way through school. The class was seated by Mr. H when we got there on the first day. We had three C names, one B name, one F name, and one P name. There were four rows that had all the football players, cheerleaders, basketball players, and baseball players—and all of them carried their noses in the air.

We had been watching Mr. H, and during test time we could see students cheating and Mr. H would be looking. All the brains in class were passing cheat notes around and Mr. H was looking right at it; but he kept smiling and kept walking, doing nothing, saying nothing. During one test, a girl pulled out the history book and looked the answer up, and Mr. H just smiled and kept walking.

We had been noticing that the teacher was giving out better grades to the other students. I knew it was going to be too close for comfort if he kept grading the way he was, marking us down and giving the better grades to the elite. I started to study real hard. One day in class he was having daily grades given on the questions he asked in class. He asked a question no one could answer, so I held up my hand and he called on me. I answered the question. He said, "I see you have been studying" and put down an A in the book. One of the cheerleaders had been reading in the book, and I saw her. She waved her hand, and Mr. H called on her. She answered the question the same way I did but changed the words around a little bit. Mr. H said, "You are right, and you are wrong, Fred." He started changing the grades in the grade book. This girl's father was the chairman of the board of education.

I could not take it anymore, and out of the desk I came. I went to the front of the room and told Mr. H that he had seen these kids cheat right in front of him and he did nothing about it. I said, "You have been downgrading all of us," and I pointed to the window row. The boys in the row jumped up and came to the front of the room and stood there with me. We demanded that he give us our grades and be fair with them, or we were going to the board of education.

All of us from the window row pointed out about the projects. We said that all of ours were original And we reminded Mr. H, "You said that the projects would be graded with the most emphasis on originality. There are projects over there you have seen in three different periods, and you have not said a word."

Mr. H said, "All of you, calm down."

The bell rang, and the elite bunch was happy and scrambling to get out of the classroom door. With the classroom empty, Mr. H said, "Give me until tomorrow to get the grades changed. Look at the grade book then; it will be lying on the desk when you come in the room tomorrow."

I said, "It better be, because I am not going to fail for anyone's mistakes."

A year later, when I was in the air force, I happened to be in the hardware store. The owner of the store, chairman of the board of education, the father of the cheerleader, was working in the store that day. I was paying off a layaway—a bow and arrow set—that my younger brother had. The cheerleader's father was running the cash register, and I told him that his daughter had cheated to get those good grades. His mouth fell open, and I walked out of the store and have never been back. Sometimes it does one good to say what is on your mind, especially when it's true. Especially if it's about a so-called high-class person. I found out years ago that everyone goes to the bathroom between two socks, that is, if you are wearing socks.

We had a big tournament at the bowling alley, and people came from all over the state to bowl in it. This meant big bucks for me. I started that morning at ten o'clock and set pins until two o'clock in the morning. We pinsetters had breaks in between when they were changing teams, and that was it. We ran and got something to eat, and we could jump any line at the snack bar. Most of the time, we ate while we were setting the pins. I set 212 games during that tournament, the most of all pinsetters. The owner had managed two other alleys, and he said no one had ever set that many before. The owner told the manager to double-check the count. He did, and it came out the same. I had to drag myself home—and I mean at a real slow walk—because I was tired. Some would say too pooped to pop or too popped to poop.

Another project that I had to make money on the side was to fix up bicycles. I started doing this when we came back from Maryland. I would round up old bicycle parts from all over and anywhere I could get them; I would put them together to make one complete bicycle, and I would sell it. I did this for the rest of my junior year and senior year. I rode a bicycle over to the thrift shop where I was going to sell it, but the man was not going to give me enough money for the bicycle, so I had to wheel and deal and swap him on some of the cost of the bicycle. I got a lighted flower arrangement for the TV for my mom and some other junk, plus money, and I was happy about the deal. While I was walking back home, I noticed something that looked like money, and it was. I picked it up; it was five dollars, and was I happy. This made the four-mile walk home a lot easier. Oh! I remember what the other junk was that I traded for. It was a lamp and a coffee-table decoration, and I gave them to my grandma. I got big hugs from my grandma, and it made me happy that she was happy about the gifts. I got myself a good pair of leather gloves. This did my hands good because they were warm; they were the first gloves that I ever had that were not cloth.

Our house became the place to gather after school in the afternoons. My dad bought a TV on credit; it was a small one called a Silvertone. Our sisters, younger brother, and all the kids in the neighborhood would gather in front of it. They would watch Mickey Mouse and Spin and Marty every afternoon in our living room—kids sitting everywhere. Sometimes I would be coming home to change clothes and get off to work. While I was changing, the laughs would be coming from the front room. Did they sound good coming from our house!

My dad got a job at the golf course when we got back from Maryland. We as a family were doing better. Dad was making more money now than he had ever made in his life. The running off and getting drunk and broke had slowed down a lot. He would slip and have a drink every now and then. I thought he did not want the neighbors to know he drank. He was a superintendent greenkeeper now. And he got my brother a job on the golf course. He learned this work real fast, and the word was he was the best greenkeeper around anywhere. He was a farmer and a nurseryman, and this fit right in with the rest of it.

The big graduation would be coming soon. Then what would be my next move? Right now I did not know, but my mind would go to the thought every now and then. I had already paid for the ring, and I was glad to get that out of the way. I knew that the money could not go anywhere else. I continued to study very hard on my history and English, and everything else took care of itself. The shop class was going good. The last project that I had time for was a cedar chest. It was a lot of work. It was going to be beautiful, with a high-gloss hand-rubbed finish on it of boiled linseed oil. The teacher said it would take six or eight coats of the linseed oil to make it high gloss. That was what I wanted, and that was what I was going to do.

Chapter 19

Graduation

We went through the graduation rehearsal. It was just a walk-through of what door to come through and where to sit down after the walk across the stage. This was a big moment for me, as I was the first in the family to graduate from high school. I knew of no one in the family on either side that had a twelfth-grade education. I was feeling good about this. I did not want to mess up and do something wrong in front of all the people that would see me walk across the stage. We had to shake hands and receive the diploma and flip the tassel from one side to the other.

The big night came, and my friend came by and picked me up. The girls were on hold until the graduation was over; then we would pick them up and do something that had not been planned yet. The graduation went fine, and there were no mess-ups; the kid that made the best grades for the whole year got to give a speech after the class president gave his speech. I think they called him a valedictorian, and he deserved a big name like that for being so smart and hanging in there when it got tough.

The speech really reached home when he said it was time to make decisions on what you were going to do for the rest of your life. It scared me a little to look at it like that—the rest of our lives. *I'm hoping that's for a long time*, I was thinking. We all stood around shaking each other's hands and hugging one another and saying, "I'll see you from time to time. Sure has been fun."

Some of these kids had been together from first grade on. They were like family. I had only two years with them, hardly that, about two months short. These kids were in one town and not bused all over the place. They saw the same kids, year after year. There had to be close feelings among the kids. They had to feel like a team and belong to one another. Even I had feelings for the school and the students. I especially remember a kid that wore his pencil down to the nub before he would go sharpen it. He was very smart and well liked. He was a great basketball player. I can remember going by his house, and he would be outside practicing basketball. Of course, I was always on my way to work or coming back from work. Little J. W. got hit by a train on the tracks, and it killed him. I have often thought about him from time to time, because I sat behind him in the third grade. My thoughts are with you, J. W. May God bless.

My friend and I rounded up the girlfriends after the graduation, and off we went to celebrate. Some of the students had invitations to some estate for a swimming party. This was for the athletes and cheerleaders and the stuck-ups. The smartest and the poorest were not invited. We would make our own fun. They were swimming, so we decided to go swimming too. That's what we did: we went to the lake to an isolated spot that was predetermined before we left school. There were five carloads, and we met at the spot and began to party. Three hours of swimming in the night air was all the girls were going to take. We came out of the water, dried off, and sat and talked to the early morning hours. What does the future hold for each of us? How long will we be knowing one another? What kind of jobs are we going to get? There was not one of us that had plans to go to college. The questions kept coming, and soon all was quiet and everyone got up and said, "I'll see you." Everyone pulled out in their cars and left.

Chapter 20

Going Air Force

I went around aimlessly for about three weeks before I made up my mind what I was going to do. I was talking to my friend and his cousin. Both had the same first name. I told them that my friend Bill, the son of my adopted grandma, told me that if I ever wanted to go into the military, the air force was the place to go. "They fly you around all over the world, and the career opportunities are better than any other branch of the military," he said. I had thought of the air force every now and then, but I had not given it a whole lot of thought until now. We three made a pact that Monday morning we were off to sign up in the air force. We went downtown and signed the papers. They gave us a piece of paper and told us we had to go to Nashville to an address and finish taking a test and doing paperwork. They told us to pack a little bag and be prepared to spend the night.

This was something new for me. Pack a small bag—what bag? All I had was a paper bag. I put a toothbrush and toiletries in the bag along with a pair of shorts and a T-shirt. I was ready now. The next afternoon I met the boys, and off we went. The plan was to go to Nashville and hang out until morning and learn the city.

When the time came to go for the tests and physical, we would be ready and close by. We all walked around the city and looked at mostly the downtown area until we were worn out from the slow walking. We decided that we were tired, and to the car we went. A nap would suit us just fine, so we tried to go to sleep in the car. Horns would blow, and the noise from the city kept us from going to sleep. After two hours of this, I got out of the car and said, "I'm going for a walk." I walked downtown and came to a parking lot that had six floors.

I walked on up to the office and spoke to the attendant; we got to talking. I was asking questions about the parking lot. "How does it work?... I bet you do a lot of walking, don't you?"

He said, "Not that much ... see the elevator?"

I looked but did not see it. He said it was a one-man elevator and pointed to it.

I asked, "How does it work?" and he showed me. He rode it up one floor and rode it back down. He jumped off on the first floor, and the belt with the steps on it went on down under the first floor. He said, "When you get to the sixth floor, be ready to jump or step off quickly." He said it was the same thing on each floor—"Just step off."

I tried this up one floor and back down. It was fun to ride this thing. I asked him if I could ride it to the sixth floor and back. He said okay. I jumped on the moving steps, and up I went. The floors had been marked with red paint in numbers to tell what floor was coming up. I got this turned around in my head somehow, and the six was on me real fast. I was only about halfway to the top to the end of the belt where it rolled over and went back down. I jumped when I saw all of that stuff in the ceiling and hit the floor and rolled. This made me nervous, and I had to walk around awhile and get my thoughts back together. I did. I knew I had to ride this thing back to the ground floor. To ride the elevator down, you had to go to the other side where the steps were going down and step on. I stepped on the moving steps, and down I went. When I saw the number two, I knew the next floor I saw would be one and I should step off. I did. When you had your timing right, this thing was fun. I went back and told my friends about it and showed it to them, but they would not ride it.

It was time to go eat breakfast. We got some food and asked for directions at the same time. We went to the address, signed in, and were told to wait. We were finally called, and they put us in a testing room. We took test after test after test. My friend acted like he was sick and fell asleep taking the test. Yes, he chickened out and was turned down because he did not finish the tests. The cousin tried to go into the army and did not make it because his urine was no good. He told me that I would have to fill up his bottle, too, so he could get in the air force. I told him okay. When it came time to fill up the bottle, they walked us in a bathroom that had a long urinal with a little shelf for the bottle. They had three people watching us, and we both said "better not" by just looking at each other. He failed, and I was by myself. I was going through with the program if I could.

My friend dropping out got me to thinking. He was in love and wanted to get married. He was afraid of losing his girl if he went in the air force. These tests couldn't be failed; they were set up to see what skills you have so they would put you in a field that you would excel in. A field of labor that you liked. You know the old saying, "You work best if you like the work." My friends returned home, and I stayed the next two nights and one and a half days and took the physical examination and passed with very good health. They told me to go home and wait on the orders to come in. Then an officer of the air force came into the room and called for attention. They passed around little Bibles, and each of us held our hands on the Bibles. We all said the oath, and the officer said, "All of you are in the air force as of right now. Go home and wait on your orders."

I knew that it would not be long before they called me to training and active duty. I had to get all of my ducks in a row before I went. I had to keep the papers in a safe place and pack no more than the list told me. They told me to have at least twenty dollars to make it to the first payday, and I did, but that was all. The class ring and the rental gown and the class dance and the good clothes I had bought to graduate in took just about all my money. I went around hugging everyone that meant something to me and the ones that I would miss most and said good-bye. Most of the time, for a joke, I would salute while saying, "Off into the wild blue yonder." I told my mom to keep my things that I had packed up in a old cardboard box and to keep my cedar chest, the one I had just made, in safekeeping until I got back.

I went to Lackland Air Force Base and started my training. The exercises and getting in shape were easy for me. I had been running and riding the bicycle for the past year and six months four nights a week and using it on the weekends to get around. My physical work came at the nursery and in the bowling alley. I was in shape—and long-winded, as you can tell. Ha!

The all-night march, which was twelve miles long with a rest halfway and at double time with a forty-pound backpack, was something else. I did not know myself when I started what I had already done physically. But on the way back, I found out this was a breeze; I was not tired, and I liked it. The other fellows were making a big deal of it and mouthing off and getting tired. I liked running, and when I got my pace set, I did not want to slow down for anyone. I was passing the big boys up. I was the last of the line in one of the two columns. I was the shortest—and proud to say, I'm five foot and seven inches tall; just over if you let me stretch out. Somehow I grew two inches in the junior and senior year, and I now weighed 137 pounds.

The night march was going good, I thought, but I wanted to get it over with. I had passed everyone up in line and was in third place. I could hear footsteps behind me; the big boots hit the ground harder and harder, and I knew everyone was getting tired. The sergeant would say how much distance we had left and ask, "Do you want to finish it off?" Everyone else was saying no, and I would yell out, "Yes, let's go for it." The sergeant would repeat himself and get the same response, and on the end I would yell out, "Yes, let's go for it." The sergeant was now using this to motivate the troops. He would run backward between the two columns and just turn to run forward as I yelled out, "Yes, let's go for it."

One of the troops was behind me now; he had been in front of me before I moved past him. This must have made him mad because he hit my backpack, knocking me forward. I kept running and digging out with my legs; one hand hit the ground, but I got back on my feet and back in stride. I said to him, "What is wrong? Aren't you man enough to take it?" The sergeant must have heard the hit on my backpack and the exchange between the troop and me. The sergeant was now running backward. He looked at me and said, "Do you want to go all the way?" I said yes, but there were a few no's. He went up and down the line from the front to the end and was telling them that the little fellow in front wanted to run all the way. "Are you going to let him outrun you? If you let him outrun you and you don't make it to the finish line, all of you will be called girls for the rest of your basic training." This was the polite way of saying it. The sergeant kept this up, and everyone kept running.

The troops were fired up and they were mad at me, but you know me by now—it did not bother me. I kept running, and we went all the way. Ninety percent of the squadron came in and took the finish line. I was first, and I felt good about it. The sergeant went around real quick and did a head count, and then he was off to report the count. When he came back, he said for all of us to gather around him, that he had something to tell us. The sergeant said we had just set the squadron record and the second-best record ever on the base since the beginning of basic training there. Cheers and yells went up; there was clapping and congratulations and handshaking, and everyone was celebrating. Then the sergeant said, "If anyone has a beef with this airman … come on up here, Airman Campbell. Take a good look at him. If you have a beef at this airman, let's hear it now. If you have a beef later, I will personally kick your butt. This airman made it possible for our squadron to break records today. Plus I have been wanting to beat Sergeant Johnson in the money pool for a long time. We, the sergeants, put five hundred dollars apiece in the pot, and the winner takes all."

The sergeant said, "Get with me later in the week." When we got together, he talked about where I learned all the things and how I was good at them. The sergeant said, "You swing from the rope like a natural; and the foot log is no problem. You climb the ropes over the bluffs, walk the tightwire, crawl under the barbed wire, shoot the rifle like an expert—where did you learn all of this?"

I explained, "I was a farm boy on and off, and started working full-time at a nursery at ten and a half years old. Swinging from the rope we learned by swimming in the creeks; we boys would climb a tree called a sapling because of its size, go all the way to the top, and start swinging back and forth and bend the sapling to the ground. At the same time, two of us would let go; the other was off for a ride back up and back and forth until the tree stopped swinging. The trick was to get a scissors hold with your legs and wrap your arms in a bear hug around one another for a good hold that would not come loose."

The sergeant laughed and shook my hand and was off. He had a French name that I can't spell, so Sergeant will have to do.

I shot an expert on the rifle range and had fun shooting the bull's-eyes. I learned how to shoot using a .22 rifle. When we went camping with Dad, he would carry the rifle and teach us boys how to shoot. This I still do. I shoot skeet, sporting clays, and trap. I have a range set up on my place and shoot quite often.

The basic training was coming to a close, and I was glad. I wanted to go on to something new. New challenges, things I had not done, and places I had not been.

We had to wait three weeks for the orders to come in. These orders would tell us what career field we would be put in and where we would go for the training. During this time, it was writing letters home and marching to chow and back. We would go out on paper pickup detail, called policing the area, almost every day or go to the Green Monster Building for more shots and some more paperwork. A runner from the squad office came by and had a note for me to come to the office. I followed him to the office. He told me to sit down and when called in to the office, to report to the captain. I did this, and the captain replied, "At ease."

The captain said, "Do you know this man?" and pointed to the man in the corner. I said no. The captain said, "Look again," and I did. But it was the same answer: "I don't know him." The captain asked, "Do you have a cousin named Junior?" I asked, "From where?" The captain asked Junior, and he said he was from Georgia. Then I said, "Yes, I know who it is."

The captain told us we could go outside and visit, for me to take as long as needed. I told Junior that he had changed so much that I did not recognize him. I said, "The last time I saw you was when you were wearing a cast and sling for your arm." He laughed and said, "That was when I broke my collarbone." I said, "You were using blue jeans material for the wads for the black powder gun. Uncle was telling you that it would blow up, and you would not listen." Junior said, "Well, it did blow up, and Dad would not help me; he turned and went back in the shop. Mom had to help me, and she was asking Dad to come and help. Uncle said, 'He would not listen to me, like he knew everything, so let him help himself or you help him.'" We both laughed and talked about everything while we drank cokes. Junior said he was in the air force and married a girl and stayed in Texas. Her father set him up in the construction business, and he was doing quite well. He did a lot of contracts for the air force here on the base. He said he was looking at the roster and saw my name and came looking for me. Junior's mom was the one that wanted to take my mother's military check and pay the bills while we were in Georgia.

Chapter 21

Parachute Training

The orders came in, and I was going to be in parachutes. For my training I would be stationed at Chanute Air Force Base, Rantoul, Illinois. The next day there were two busloads, about seventy-two of us and our bags. They took us to San Antonio, Texas, and put us on a train called the Missouri Pacific Railroad, and we were on our way to our new place of learning. They let us off at Champaign, Illinois, and bused us on in to Chanute Air Force Base. We were in training. We marched to and from meals and to the classrooms, and we worked. We had to learn how to take a parachute completely apart and put it back together. The same thing for sewing machines. You had to learn how to sew nylon that was even and smooth and make perfect patches before you could graduate the school. I found the secret: don't be afraid to work with it; handle it just like you would any other material; have the machine set properly and sew away, and you could sew the perfect patch. I had a friend that could not catch on, and I told him the secret. He sewed the patch just in time not to be extended over into the next class. He was thankful, and we got shipped out to different places.

The winters were the coldest I had ever been in for such a long time. Snow, more than I had ever seen before, was on the ground, and it stayed on the ground until melted by the sunshine. We had to march on it every day that it laid there. Then it was time for flu shots. We had to get the shot and then report for our paychecks. There were airmen lying everywhere in the dayroom and outside on the ground. They were passing out, and some were screaming with big tears in their eyes. My arm felt like it fell off; it knotted up in a muscle cramp and hurt like hell, but I got paid and walked out. Word got around that this was not to be done anymore because it took three hours longer for the payroll to be finished.

I got to running track and training for a twelve-mile race. An airman named Carroll—last name—and I would go and run at night for about two hours of training. The time came for the big race, and we had to stand barracks inspection. We were standing there in our running shorts for the inspection and trying to explain we had signed to run in the race. The captain would not excuse us, and the race was over by the time we came out of the barracks.

I'm directing my attention in a different direction from now on if this is the way it is with sports. Wasted training; effort was lost, and nothing was gained.

We had to pull barracks guard duty every so often. Every now and then, some of the airmen did not want to pull their shift, and I would hire out to pull their duty. I saved this money to buy a car someday. One morning I was standing barracks guard duty; it was cold, and the snow was still on the ground. I was looking out the door every once in a while like we were taught to do and making the rounds upstairs and checking if the doors were still locked and everything was okay. I looked up, and a cat came up in front of the door and started to hang around. Remember, it was cold and there was snow on the ground. I felt sorry for this cat and decided it needed help. I opened the door, and the cat came to me; I closed the door very quietly and petted the cat and settled it down. Then I went and put the cat down under the cover on the bunk closest to me, and the cat went down to the foot of the bed and lay still. I went to wake up my replacement and got off duty. I went straight to bed because I wanted to get the one hour of sleep that was left before we had to get up.

The barracks guard gave the wake-up alarm, and everyone started getting up. Then the screaming and jumping began. One airman was using the bunks for trampolines and hitting his head on the ceiling and was six bunks away from his bunk. He was almost white, and he was a black airman. His eyes were very, very big—I mean big. He was shaking all over while two airmen held him. Someone went and jerked the cover back on the bunk and found the cat under the cover. The airman had a boot in his hand not knowing what was under the cover. He picked the cat up and said, "It's just a kitty cat, Airman Miller. Do you want to pet it?" The airman went to screaming and shaking again. The barracks chief asked me about the cat, and I said, "I don't know anything about it. Everything was okay when I went to bed." Looking back, I'm glad it was Airman Miller—he was a smart butt from Chicago.

Chapter 22

Little Rock Static

The orders came in, and I was going to Little Rock, Arkansas. I thumbed my way home to save money; this means to hitch a ride that's free. With the uniform on, it was no problem. One ride, then another one after the other, and then I was in Tennessee. I was taking just one week off and then going to Little Rock and reporting in for duty. Little Rock was a huge air base and had one of the biggest airstrips. The B-52 could land and take off there. That would be one of my duties once I learned how to pack the drag chutes.

They assigned me to the personal chute division and started training me to get my first grade level. The grade levels are one, three, five, and seven and designate how much you know about your job. The training went great. I had a instructor that worked with me all morning, leaving the afternoon for classes. I had learned how to study just before getting out of high school, and applying it here worked really good. The learning came a lot easier once I knew how to study.

The one level, where we were now working, did not require a test. The three level required passing a test. There were three students from each squadron being taught by the same instructors. Since there were two squadrons on base, six people were going to take the test at the same time. I ran the class every once in a while when Sergeant Fritts was on appointments for whatever. All six of us went to the squadron office and had a trial run over what to expect when we took the test. The squadron officer sat in on the class and was very impressed; he shook hands with each of us and said, "You people are going to do just fine on the test." That was true; I scored the highest grade ever for our squadron and second highest ever on the base. This meant a shop party, and it was quite a party.

I continued with the training and enjoyed packing the chutes. Each step was critical so the chute would open each time the pilot pulled the rip cord. Our pilots depended on the parachute riggers to do the job right 100 percent of the time. I gave these procedures every ounce of my attention and practiced until I could do the job as well as, if not better than, the instructor. My chutes were neat and uniform each and every time. I had confidence in my work and believed that any of my chutes would open if needed to save a life.

There was a big tower that was used for hanging chutes in to dry them. Each one of the chutes was a different weight. The big B-52 chute weighed 107 pounds. The fighter plane drag chutes were smaller, and weight was according to size. The personal chute and chest chute weighed a lot less. The chutes, when wet, would weigh three times their dry weight. I washed one of the personal chutes and was going to hang it up for drying. I hooked the apex of the chute up and started pulling down on the rope to pull the chute up. Keep in mind that I only weighed 137 pounds. The higher up the tower the chute went, the more it weighed as it came off the ground. First thing I knew was that my feet were no longer touching the floor. I was riding the rope and swinging around having fun. I would jump up and start hand over hand climbing the rope and going higher and higher. Each time the ride was longer and longer, going about fifty feet in the air and back down. I had it up about halfway and was swinging to one side trying to get to a hook and tie the rope off. After three tries my hands slipped on the rope, and the chute began coming down at a high rate of speed. I was thinking I should get away from it and just let it fall; I tried to run, but the rope curled out and grabbed my arm, giving me rope burns all over my left arm. The chute just missed me, and my arm was burning and the skin was missing around my arm in three places.

I went to the first-aid box and got what I needed to put on the burns. My instructor asked what was going on, and I told him. He laughed, and I laughed with him. The tower was 125 feet tall. The instructor said, "Everyone needs help to hang a chute, and you should have been told that."

I continued my training until I had learned all that was needed to be learned, according to the instructor. So the next move was to go to the drag chutes shop and learn to pack and maintain the drag chutes. The big B-52 chute had to be pulled out, untangled, and stretched out before packing could begin. I grabbed the chute by the apex and pulled it out. They said, "That's the way to do it, but next time, run and do the pull on the run." The next time came, and the instructor told me to take the coupling end. That is the part that hooks onto the plane. It's made of heavy metal. The weather had been hot, and the chutes had been laying on the runway; when the runway was cleared of planes, they were picked up and brought to the hanger for packing. The hanger was big and a breeze blew through it almost every day, which made it cool and created great working conditions.

The instructor had said to me, "Go pull it on the run," so I did. I ran and pulled; and just before I got to the end, a ball of fire hit my hand and went up my arm. I screamed and yelled out loud, and it almost knocked me down. *What was that?* I was slapping my arm to get the feeling back into it. Everyone in the shop was laughing and pointed at me and laughed some more. The instructor said, "It's static electricity. It builds up when a hot chute is pulled over a cool floor and the fabrics rub together; this makes the static electricity." I said, "It's hot." Everyone laughed, and the training continued.

One day the word came down that one of our fighter planes had crashed. They said the pilot was okay; he had bailed out, and the chute opened perfectly. Every one of us was glad the pilot was okay. The next day the records were checked on the chute that was used, and the instructor's name and my name were on the paperwork. Since I was in training, I did not get credit for the packing of the chute nor was I awarded a certificate. But the instructor shook my hand and said, "Job well done." Everyone congratulated me.

The rules were that if you are not certified at the grade level, you could not be held responsible. The lieutenant pilot of the plane brought a fifth of whiskey by the shop and gave it to the instructor. The lieutenant pilot thanked us and was grateful that I had been working in the drag chute shop. Saving someone's life was at the top of the list of good things to help people. The shop chief said we could have a party Friday after work. Everyone was looking forward to it, even me.

Remember the cat and the airman named Miller in Illinois? They had transferred him to Little Rock. When I saw him, I asked, "What are you doing here?" He said they got his orders messed up and sent him where he was not needed. I told him that I had forgotten about the cat—that is, if he would behave and not be a smart butt. We agreed and were on our way to being good friends.

Miller was assigned to the drag chute packing, and the instructor started him on the same procedures that he had started me on. The instructor winked at me; I smiled and kept on working. Miller weighed less than I weighed. The trial run was not too good. The instructor had to explain that speed was important, and the faster you run, the faster the chute would untangle. The instructor exchanged the ends of the chutes. He handed Miller the coupler and said, "Run, I mean run with it, pull as hard as you run." By this time Miller was pumped up and was digging out.

Being from Chicago, Airman Miller wanted to impress everyone he met. So he was giving it his all. When he got to the end, the electricity popped him in the same manner that it did me. Airman Miller squealed, screamed, and hit the floor. He rolled over twice and lay there and started shaking; then he jumped to his feet. Airman Miller's eyes were big, and he cussed and walked out of the shop. He went to the street, and the staff sergeant went after him. They talked and came back in; we were all still laughing. He pointed his finger at me and said, "You knew this would happen to me." I said yes and started laughing again, and everyone joined in. This time Airman Miller joined in too. I told Airman Miller this was pulled on every new man when they came in and they had gotten me good.

Chapter 23

Off into the Wild Blue Yonder

Orders came in for an airman in the other squadron to go to Germany. The airman did not want to go. I told him I would go for him if I could, and for him to go check it out with headquarters and get back with me. The airman came back and said nothing could be done. I went to headquarters and talked to the head man and asked him for help. He said I was a three level, and the orders asked for a one level. I explained that I had passed the test but had not gotten the orders, so that made me still a level one. He told me to go see the base commander and report in to him.

I did just that, and the commander asked, "Why do you want to go to Germany?"

I told him, "The sign said join the air force and see the world. I've seen training bases and some states, and that's it so far."

The commander asked, "Who is the girl that you got pregnant?"

I said, "There is no pregnant girl, sir."

The commander said, "Do you owe a lot of money, airman?"

I said, "No sir, I just want to see some of the world."

The commander said, "You will have to extend the length of service you have left, because the tour to Germany is three years."

I said, "Yes, sir. How do I do that?"

The commander said, "I'll fix up the paperwork, and you go to chow. When you get back here, we will let you walk the paperwork through the system step by step."

I did just that, and at the end of the day I had orders cut and leave papers. I had three days to get my personal stuff done and go on leave before I would leave the country. The other airman was relieved and thankful that he did not have to go.

Something kept telling me that I should go to Germany when I heard the other airman did not want to go. It was bugging me for two days. As soon as I knew I was going, the feeling was gone. I went home, said my good-byes to all of my friends, and told each of them that I was off the see the world. I told my mom to hang onto the stuff I had stored and to keep the cedar chest for me until I got back. The last week of my leave time, I was off to see my older brother, who was still in Maryland. My brother and I hung out and talked about old times. I had not seen my brother in three years, since the family moved back to Tennessee. After my visit, my brother took me to the bus station, and I got on the bus for McGuire Air Force Base in New Jersey, where I would catch the plane for Frankfurt, Germany. I was thinking the world waits on anyone who wants to see it. But you shouldn't wait too long, or you will be too old to enjoy the view. While I was growing up, I knew there was better to be had; it was just a matter of finding it. I was looking for the better in everything I saw and did. I hoped I had made the right decision and would find what I was looking for.

Then my thoughts went to the airplane ride. I had not ridden a plane before, and I wondered what it was like. I thought to myself,

Other people ride planes, so I can ride a plane too. To my surprise, the plane ride was great and I liked it. The takeoff was okay, and next was the landing in Germany.

I flew into Frankfurt, Germany, and got loaded on a bus. They took us to the chow hall. Then it was back on the bus to a big building for paperwork and tickets for a train. The bus dropped me and two other airmen off at the train station, and we were going to ride a train to Trier, Germany. The countryside was unbelievable. The beauty of this country was beyond describing for a high school boy's vocabulary.

My eyes were not missing much. The high mountains and the grapevines on the hillsides. Neat farms on each side of the railroad tracks. The railroad tracks ran along the side of the river in a lot of places. The river was clean and boats were moving, but they did not look like they were fishing. They must have been hauling something for delivery. The boats were different from any boats that I had ever seen. They still were pretty to look at. The houses were made different than the houses in America. The houses were made of stone, big rocks, and tile roofs and looked ten times as strong as anything made in America. I could tell by looking at them, they were warmer in the winter months than anything that I had lived in. The shops and stores along the way looked small and compact. In every little town, someone was moving about, going here and there about their daily chores. I was thinking there must be a lot of businessmen over there because everyone had a briefcase. The people dressed differently than Americans do. The people in the towns looked well dressed. The girls were dressed differently than our girls; and from what I could see from the train and on the train, they were pretty.

There was a girl on the train who had gotten on at a stop along the way. She came into the train car that we airmen were in. She sat down and smiled. I was thinking she was pretty; the three of us were talking about it. We tried talking to her, but she could not understand us. We made sign language, and we got her laughing. We all got quiet after awhile. She took out a box from her big sack, opened it up, and started eating candy. We watched, and she could tell that each of us wanted to taste the candy; we just knew that the candy was something that we had never tasted before. It was chocolate and had some kind of juice or syrup in it. It was good and tasty. In fact, just for the record, it was the best candy that I had ever eaten. The girl was very generous and let us eat several pieces of the candy. I gave her some money, and the other airmen put money in on it too. We thanked her; she knew what it meant and said *danke schon*.

We sat there in our seats and felt a little tipsy. We airmen were talking and agreed that's how we all felt. I said, "It feels like I drank a couple of beers." We all agreed. We asked the girl about the candy, and communication was enough to find out the candy had cognac in it. The fräulein said it was liquor from France. The fräulein's stop came up, and we thanked her as she was getting off the train.

We all took a nap and woke up with the man on the train telling us it was time to get off the train. We were in Trier, Germany, and the air force bus was waiting on us. To the base we went. The city was beautiful, and it was getting dark fast. We did not see much as the bus went up the mountain. The winding roads were dark, and we could only look where the headlights were shining.

The little towns would come and go in the town lights as the bus was going up the mountainside. We finally stopped looking and started asking questions to the bus driver. He was a lifer, and he told us to settle down and take our time. He said, "You will be learning new things for a long while."

Chapter 24

A Very Good Feeling

The U.S. Army and the U.S. Air Force shared the base outside the town of Spangdahlem, Germany. This would be my home for the next three years.

I got settled in after the long paper trail of processing in. It takes about three days of going around the base and signing in to get the paperwork done. Reporting for duty was slow in coming because we had to wait the weekend plus Monday, which was a holiday and everyone was off. We were put up in the temporary barracks and given temporary meal cards until Monday. We needed the rest after the fourteen hours on the plane and the long train ride to get here. We rested all right; we changed our minds and went back to Frankfurt. It was coming up to New Year's, and we did not want to miss it. We three caught the train and off we went. In Frankfurt we tried to get a hotel room but could not. Every hotel was full up. The man in the hotel called around, but everywhere was the same thing: no rooms of any kind. We decided to go party and sleep on the street or in a bar or whatever.

The bars were huge; I had never seen anything like this before. The bars were called guesthouses, and we found the biggest in Frankfurt—although we didn't know it at the time. The guesthouse had a balcony, and another balcony above that balcony, but smaller. There were pretty women and girls carrying beer in both hands; they had the prettiest dresses on. There was a huge dance floor to the rear of the first floor, and the band was above, on the stage . The band had on little leather britches with shoulder straps. I did not know what they were playing, but it did not matter because it was real good music that I liked. We finally got someone to bring us a beer; we had to stand and drink the beer. The beer mug was large, with a lot of beer in it, and it lasted for a spell. We ordered again. Drinking the second beer, we got to discussing our finances. We were all running low, so we backed off of the beer drinking and just enjoyed the music and the sights in the biggest bar we had ever been in. Three strangers in a strange land—even if we could have spoken German, we would not have talked because we were so busy looking, enjoying every minute of it.

We were just about to call it a night and leave when the band went crazy and started slapping one another around. The leather britches were popping from the slaps, and some of them were chopping wood and yelling out in high-pitched voices. We stayed. We did not want to miss any of this. We did not order any more beer. When it was over, I knew that we had enjoyed it and would be talking about it for a lifetime. I had figured out the slapping each other around was part of the show, and we got a good laugh out of it.

Back on the street, we spent the next hour walking around taking in the sights. Then back to the bar for the New Year to come in. All the people cheered and hugged each other. We said happy New Year to each other, and the focus was where to go from here. During the hour we had heard sirens go off three times. We had no place to sleep, so we went to the train depot and got tickets for the return trip to the base.

I found a spot in the train station where I could sit down, see the schedule board, and see the clock at the same time. The two other airmen liked the idea and followed suit. It was a two-hour wait before the train came in. We got a little rest. Once we got on the train and got seated, we fell asleep. Since it was early morning and we were tired from being up all night, we slept almost the entire trip to Trier. Once the train arrived, we got a taxicab—a Mercedes-Benz—and we were off, and I do mean off. This man was crazy and drove like a madman. Up the mountain we went at a high rate of speed, making the tires cry on every curve. One of us was up front, and I and the other were in the backseat. We were sliding back and forth from one side of the car to the other. You know, from door to door. We thought it was fun, but we were worried a bit too. When we got to the top of the mountain and leveled out, a smooth ride took over; that made the ride a pleasant trip.

We finished checking in and made the move from the temporary barracks to the barracks that would be our home. The next day I checked in at the parachute shop and was ready for duty. When all of my records caught up to me, the shop chief studied them. Seeing my test scores, he made me the new instructor. It was going to be easy for me to put together a class. I had kept all of my study papers and notes. I held class and taught packing the chutes and repairs. I had only two students, and they were smart people and easy to teach. All they needed was practice and more practice. It came time for them to take the test. When the orders came down and they both had passed, each of them thanked me and treated me to some beers at the Airmen's Club.

When I was not teaching, I had to work at packing the chutes like everyone else. The chutes had to be packed every third month. We opened them up, aired them out, inspected them, and repacked them. So there was never-ending work. On March 19, 1960, we heard that one of our fighter planes had gone down. It was an emergency ejection from the plane. The word was that the pilot was okay; the chute had worked. The chute was brought in, and I had packed it. Two days later Captain C. Mason came by the shop and found me. He had a forty-ounce bottle of bourbon whiskey. He thanked me several times and shook my hand. I was very pleased with the attention that I was getting.

We partied, and then it was back to work as normal. I was trying to take German in classes on base. Here came a big envelope with my name on it. It was a certificate of merit from the Caterpillar Club honoring me for work well done and for saving the life of one of our pilots. The certificate was from the Switlik Parachute Co. in Trenton, New Jersey. I felt like I was six feet tall for a couple weeks, and I walked around standing tall.

Certificate of Merit

FRED W. CAMPBELL

is honored by the Caterpillar Club for his vigilant maintenance of safety equipment. On MARCH 19, 1960 a parachute he serviced was used in an emergency to save the life of C. C. Mason

President

SWITLIK
PARACHUTE CO.
TRENTON, NEW JERSEY

The time came to start looking at everything that was around me. This was a beautiful country, and I needed to see it and take in its beauty. I had become friends with an airman named Bill, short for William. We started going to town just outside the base gate and drinking a few beers and learning the culture. We needed to learn how to order food and ask questions about where to go. The counting of money was easy to learn because we were spending money every time we went to town. I dropped out of the German classes on base because the instructor, the so-called teacher, went too fast and definitely could not get the job done on me.

I bought a car—a rocket '88 Oldsmobile, black in color; it was a good running car. We started going a little farther from the base each time out. I took in the glider plane show, and it was something else. I planned trips to Luxemburg. I would line up three airmen that wanted to go, and I would charge them a fee for the ride down and back. I went to Belgium with a friend to pick up a car, a Buick, that he had bought and drove back the car that we went in. It surprised me that there were American cars over there and they were export models.

I went to Amsterdam, Holland. This was out of the world! There were naked girls gazing from open windows along the canal streets. Most of the people could speak English. The boats moving around in the city were quite a sight for this youngster. Four of us airmen rented bicycles and went riding in the city and checking out the landmarks. The architecture of the buildings and of the churches was the most beautiful that I had ever seen. The city was beautiful everywhere we looked. The city was clean, and the people friendly—what more could a visitor want?

We stopped for a bit to eat and rest up. From school we knew there was an ocean around somewhere. I asked the waitress, and she said it was about ten kilometers and pointed the way. We got back about an hour before dark, and the bicycle shop was just about closing up when we got there. We were tired, worn-out, and hungry and needed a shower and clean clothes.

I got to Paris, France, twice. It was a great city, though both the streets and the people were dirty. Meat hung outside of shops, with flies all over the meat. Most of the people were nice. A few people would see the car plate and know we were Americans; they showed us how intelligent they were by sticking up their middle finger at us as they passed us on the highway. Two people passed us on a motorcycle, and the finger came up as they passed. We had an opening on a long stretch of road, so Steve suggested catching and passing them up. He said he wanted to give them an apple. I thought he was going to hand them an apple as we went by, but that is not what he meant. His arm went out the window, and he hook shot the apple over the car in front of the motorcycle; the apple hit the driver in the chest, knocking the breath out of him. The driver's feet fell to the ground, and they pulled off the road. The motorcycle later caught back up with us, but they showed no fingers and stayed behind us until they turned off.

I was picked to march in a parade in Luxembourg. It was for a big May Day celebration. All the armed forces of America were represented: Army, Navy, Marines, and the Air Force.

I took note that the countries of Germany, Luxembourg, Belgium, Holland, France, and Austria were all represented. All of the people were very respectful, grateful, and very happy to take part in the celebration. The parachute shop had a display under a tent for the spectators, where we would describe and let the people look at the different kinds of chutes. Everybody was marching down the street, one group after the other, all branches of service. The cheers came for us Americans. It made chill bumps come up on my arms. It was a great feeling that I will never forget.

Going through the center of town with big buildings on each side was like walking along a narrow balcony. People were hanging out the windows yelling and cheering. As we marched, the squads up front would get the cheers first, and then they passed on down the line. We could hear the cheers everywhere. When we went through, our cheers were the loudest. It made us proud to be in the air force, serving our country.

Our base was seven minutes from the Russian border by airplane. We had base alerts all the time and constantly practiced what to do. They set me up on a team to get on a truck loaded with the chutes and everything needed to open up a new base in case of attack. We would go as fast as we could go to France and open up an old base, set up shop, and be ready for our fighter planes to come in after making a run. Most times it was a three-day exercise.

Every forty-five to sixty days during the winter months, when fog was part of the weather for Germany, we would have TDY— temporary duty assignment. The TDY was to take place in Libya, the land of sunshine. We got extra pay for this assignment. I would take the trip about twice a year, and it was good to get away from the cold winter weather. We would go swimming in the Mediterranean Sea and lie around and rest up for a while. I went on trips to see the Roman ruins and take in the sights of the sand. I saw my first octopus while walking on the beach. An old man from Libya was hunting for them and running his hands under rocks and back in holes along the beach.

The third or fourth time down to Libya, I was looking for new things to do. I had heard about the horse-riding trail. I would go horseback riding Arab style. I was a mule rider, but they ride the same as a horse. This was fun; if you were lucky, you got a horse that was full of sprit and energy. I found one horse and we got along good; I would ask for him. This made the forty-five days slip by fast. I took four rides, one a week. I brought a couple of cookies to give to the horse, one before and one after the ride. The small horses were fast and fun to ride. The sand made the saddle set easy all the time. The hard ground would be a different story.

I saw a golf course from the road, and this game was next on my list of things to do. One of the airmen from jet engines was talking to me, just idle talk, and I asked him if he had ever played golf. He said he had a couple of times. I asked if he would show me how to play, and he agreed. I had just gotten my hair cut into a flattop. I never wore a cap except while on duty. We were off to play golf, and not thinking, I didn't wear a cap. We played one round and then another, which was eighteen holes that afternoon. My head blistered, and the flattop gel melted and ran all over my head, down behind the ears and down the neckline. What a mess! In four days, my skin was peeling off the top of my head. It was like scaling a fish or having dandruff that was coming off as big as snowflakes. I never played golf again. I hit a few balls along the way, but no more golf.

The living conditions in downtown Libya, Tripoli, were terrible. One part of town was nice and clean-looking; on the other side was a slum, with waste running down the center of the street. This part of town was off-limits to everyone. These people would kill at the drop of a hat. The business district was where tapestries were available. I bought several and sent them home to America, in care of my mom.

Chapter 25

Dream Girl

Back in Germany, I started going to the city of Trier, which was the biggest and closest city around. It is the oldest city in Germany. It dates back to the Roman Empire. In fact, the Romans occupied Trier at one time. Some of the Roman ruins are still there. It is a beautiful city, and the river Mosel runs alongside of the city. There are castles on top of the mountain and plenty of things to see and visit. I loved the city, and the girls were pretty.

My friend Frank was from New York State. He would hitch a ride with me into town, and I would not see him again until time to leave. He was going with a fräulein. She never came to the guesthouses. I asked Frank about that, and he told me that she had been married, had two children, and worked in a factory. I asked him, "Does she have a girlfriend? Find out and get me a date, okay?"

That happened, and I met this girl and started dating her. We hit it off real good. We did everything together. We went sightseeing, partying, bowling, wine feasts, for long walks, and swimming in the river where the bombs fell and blew out big holes in the river. We went to Oktoberfests everywhere we could.

Helga was her name, and we have been together forty-eight years; we married, and we are still going everywhere together. Looking back, I realize I was wanting to go to Germany and could not get it off my mind until I knew I was going. This is why I wanted to go to Germany: she was waiting on me to show up.

Helga's grandmother lived on the side of the river, and we could see the house from where we were swimming. In the summer months we sat at night and drank beer in a little picnic area outside the house. We could see the river and the boats' lights as we sat and talked. Helga was working at a cigarette factory, and I would wait at Oma's house for her to come home from work. Oma taught me to drink coffee and to like it. She had a handheld coffee grinder. Oma taught me how to put my knees together and hold the grinder while I ground the coffee. I had my little dictionary and would look up words as we made conversation. The book translated English to German on the most commonly used words.

Helga was born in this house and grew up mostly with her grandmother. I stayed over several nights at the house; I stayed in the front part of the house where there was heat. This was the living room and dining room area. One night when the weather was so bad I did not try to go back to the base, I stayed in the bedroom. The bed was feathers and soft; I sank into the bed, and wrapped the feather tick around me. Oma put another feather tick over the top of me and sealed me in for the night. This was the best and warmest bed that I had ever slept in. There was no heat of any kind in the back rooms of the house.

I had made a friend of Oma and loved her for her kindness and her love for her granddaughter. Oma knew I loved Helga and I would take care of her. I could tell by the way she looked at me with the warmest smile. I will never forget this wonderful woman.

Chapter 26

Mutual Commitments

I knew I needed to start getting ready for something, but just what I did not have a grip on. I started saving my money and buying the best of clothes. I liked the sweaters that were made in Germany. I bought fifteen of them, all different colors and kinds. Some were for winter, and others were for spring and fall.

I signed up for the TDY trip again. The extra pay, which was one dollar and forty-five cents a day, would come in handy. I stayed sixty-two days this time. Headquarters got the orders messed up, and the replacements did not show up.

I played poker every weekend, both Friday and Saturday nights. I played mostly blackjack and got good at the game; I'm sure I was lucky too. I saved the money.

I got lonely, though; something was missing again. I knew I missed Helga and Germany. I was looking forward to getting back and getting my feelings straightened out. I came back each time with a tan and my hair white and blond as it could be. New people on base would look and wonder where I got the tan. German people just could not get a grip on the tan; I was almost copper color.

The May Day celebration would be on our base this time. I asked Helga to come, and she did. I showed the planes off to her and explained the job I did. We watched the parade, got something to eat, and sat and talked. We had a good time. After that I found out I could get a visitor pass so she could come on base and go to the movies, bowling, and snack bars. We were going bowling in a small town outside of Trier. This was German bowling, with small pins. I wanted to show her the big pins and the big ball—American-style bowling. In the bowling alley I got everything set up, and we began to bowl; I showed her how to put her fingers in the ball. Helga was making the swing and released it on the back of the swing. The ball came at me going backward from her, and I had to catch it. We had a big laugh about it and still laugh about the good time we had.

Helga and I went to Amsterdam, Holland, for the Tulip Fest. This was the most flowers that I had ever seen. Going into the country, crossing the border, both sides of the road—there were flowers everywhere. All around the windmills in the front yards, along the canals, and everywhere you looked, there were tulips. I took Helga on a tour boat through the canals. There was a lot to be seen from the boat. She said that she enjoyed the trip very much and would never forget it.

We ate breakfast at a fancy restaurant, where the waiter was taking very good care of us. He brought out some eggs in a little holder, like a pedestal for the eggs to sit on. I had never seen this before. I told Helga that I could peel the eggs really fast, faster that anyone else. "I will show you." She tried to tell me the eggs were not for peeling; the top comes off, and you eat out of the shell. With her not being able to speak English and me not understanding German very well, I did not comprehend what she was saying. I grabbed the egg and hit both ends on the table. I peeled off the ends and put the egg to my mouth and was going to blow the egg out of the hull. I blew—and the egg went everywhere, all over the white tablecloth, the floor, us, and down the front of my shirt. The waiter ran out and saw what was happening, and everyone laughed. He said it was okay and started to change the tablecloth, the dishes, and everything. I had never eaten a soft-boiled egg and had not heard of them either. I was embarrassed, and my face was bright red. On the ride back from Holland, Helga had never laughed so hard. I laughed with her and at myself for my lack of knowledge of a soft-boiled egg.

I certainly know how tipping got started. I tipped—very generously—and shook the waiter's hand. I wonder how many times the waiter has told that story while drinking or at a party.

The Cuban conflict was taking place, and alerts were given for practice once a month for about six months. We had to be ready for anything. I was still hanging at the base and not going on TDY anymore. Helga and I were dating, going to the small towns, and taking in the sights. We went to the fairs, and they were similar to ours. There were wine fests all over, along with the Oktoberfest. The whole month of October is a party month. Fasching is a lot of fun. The fräuleins dress up and cover their faces, and no one knows who is who until midnight. The masks come off, and the fun begins. You could have been dancing with your girlfriend or a boy or whomever. There are three days of partying in the month of February each year.

Remember the briefcases that everyone was carrying around, and I thought everyone worked in an office? Well, they don't. German civil service workers on the base do the painting and upkeep. I noticed that coming and going, all of them had briefcases. Then when they were painting the parachute shop, I saw them stop for lunch—and they took out lunch and a beer from their "briefcases." Most factories had a shower for the employees. The Germans would wear suits to and from work and carry their lunches in briefcases. It was funny I thought that everyone worked in an office.

President Kennedy cut my tour by two months. He said America had to cut the size of our military. I did not like this. I did not want to leave. I loved this place. I got the paperwork done on Helga and gave her a wedding band on the way back from Frankfurt. We stopped in a little town named Mainz, got matching wedding bands, and married that day.

We planned all the way back. Helga's brother was going in the German Army and serving his time. She wanted to wait on him to go in before she came to America. Together we had a plan, and it would take awhile for it to come together.

Remember the family dog that moved everywhere with us? From farm to farm. Out of state and back to our home state. This dog had the run of the neighborhood, and the neighbors loved him. He could knock on doors and visit at as many as five houses. The houses had screen doors; he would take his paw and knock on the door, and the neighbors would answer the door. They would pet him and give him some leftover breakfast. He used this system to get his treats.

In the summer months Mac was blond in color, and in the winter months he would turn red like a fox. Mac would carry his tail curled up over his back like a Siberian Husky dog. He walked proudly everywhere he went. I always thought he was my dog. I was the one that got him from under the floor of the house—twice.

I got a letter from Mom, and she told me he got shot by a boy who lived on the farm the next road over. I could not finish the letter. I was crying, and it hurt bad. I'm glad I was in Germany because I might have done something stupid. I knew this boy from school. His stairs did not go to the upper floor. I went to town and had some beer. By this time the beer tasted good to me. The music and drink helped keep my mind off of it. I finished the letter two days later and wrote my mom back. The letter told me that the whole family, the neighbors, and everyone was crying about the dog. Mac was gone and would be missed, but never forgotten.

I'm happy that so many people loved him and shared him. This helped ease my mind whenever I thought about our dog.

Chapter 27

Flight-Line Details

The parachute shop was crowded, and I had everyone up to the five level stats. I was one of the ones chosen to go on detail. The detail was to work in shops to help them catch up on the work. I started out at the paint shop and was the gofer. I helped sand and get things ready for painting.

I was put in the sheet metal shop for two weeks and then moved to the jet engine shop. Then we sanded a helicopter down and made sheet metal repairs and spray painted the primer paint on it. After that, the painter from the paint shop came and painted the helicopter. It looked new.

There was a big metal press that was in France, in the town of Etain. The NCOIC—that's the Non-Commissioned Officer in Charge—got permission to go get it. When it got to our base, the NCOIC came and got me and Steve, a good friend of mine, and wanted this machine restored. The NCOIC said, "Anything you want; go to any shop and to the tool crib. If anyone gives you a hard time and you don't get what you need, come and tell me. If you need anything machined, bring the work order to me and I will sign it."

We came in to work every day and did not report to anyone. No one bothered us, and everything went well. This metal press was a monster with hydraulics. It exerted one hundred tons of pressure. It would crimp a twelve-foot-long piece of metal three-sixteenths inch thick. We painted operating signs all over the press. We put new hydraulic lines in and took off all the rust from the pistons and put new rubber seals in the hydraulics. We cleaned every crimping blade, removing all the rust and polishing them back out to a shine. Finally it was time to put it back into service.

The NCOIC demonstrated the machine in front of everyone that worked on the flight line and the officers too. Pictures were taken. We were congratulated and our hands were shook, plus we got pats on the back and everyone saying, "Job well done." The story came out in the base paper, in the paper for Europe Armed Forces, and the paper for the U.S. military. The NCOIC was thankful and said, "If you ever need anything, just ask." This made Steve and me feel top-notch. With us being in the military, this was like having an ace in the hole.

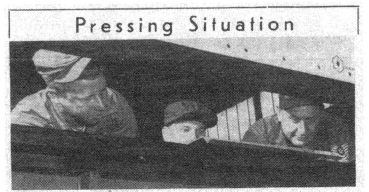

Pressing Situation

Perhaps not the recommended way of creasing a piece of paper, this hydraulic press brake nevertheless exerts up to 100 tons of pressure and can take and bend a piece of metal up to 12 feet long and 3/16" thick. The only one of its kind at a tactical fighter unit in Europe, it is demonstrated here by MSgt Raul E. Ulm, (right), Assistant NCOIC of Fabrications Branch, while the two men who refurbished it, A3C Steve R. Grooms, (left) and A2C Fred W. Campbell, look on.

Got an Iron Petticoat?
Chute Riggers Restore Hydraulic Press Brake

Need a 30,000-pound hydraulic press brake refurbished? At Spang when this problem arose, it was none other than two parachute riggers who were called upon to do the job.

Now hydraulic press maintenance doesn't quite fall under the qualifications of a parachute rigger. Even so, the job had to be done. Due to a lack of hydraulic fluid and the absence of a location for the press, it had set unused since the 49th Tactical Fighter Wing first moved to Spangdahlem from Etain Air Base, France, over a year ago. The general consensus of opinion was that it was high time the machine was back in running order.

And so, A2C Fred W. Campbell and A3C Steve R. Grooms, two parachute riggers with the 49th Materiel Section, were called upon to do the job. Within a short time the machine had been cleaned, painted, marked in accordance with the tech order and put into operational use... The only one of its kind at a tactical fighter unit in Europe.

Able to exert 100 tons of pressure, the titanic press extends 20 inches into a concrete floor in Hangar # 2 at Spang. It can take and bend a piece of metal up to 12 feet in length and has a maximum breaking capacity of 3/16".

Master Sergeant Rual E. Ulm, Assistant NCOIC of Fabrications Branch at Spang and one of the operators of the hydraulic press, was more than satisfied with its operation. "The machine is now in fine running order, thanks to the efforts of these two men; and anyone within the command who has a legitimate reason for wanting to take advantage of the press is welcome to do so," he said.

Pressing Situation

Perhaps not the recommended way of creasing a piece of paper, this hydraulic press brake nevertheless exerts up to 100 tons of pressure and can take and bend a piece of metal up to 12 feet long and 3/16" thick. The only one of its kind at a tactical fighter unit in Europe, it is demonstrated here by MSgt Raul E. Ulm, (right), Assistant NCOIC of Fabrications Branch, while the two men who refurbished it, A3C Steve R. Grooms, (left) and A2C Fred W, Campbell, look on.

After our day in the sunshine, it was back to the parachute shop; and the days seemed to get longer. My mind was wandering and thinking *I don't have long to stay in Germany now.* I spent a lot of the days looking out the window just thinking, *Where to from here? What am I going to do when Helga and I are stateside? What kind of a job will I have?* All these questions and more ran through my head.

Chapter 28

Going Home

When I joined up, the sign said, "Join the Air Force and see the world." Let's do a rundown and find out where all I have been. Germany, Holland, Belgium, France, Libya, Italy, Luxemburg, Azores Islands—that's eight countries that I have been to, and some of them were very interesting. I did get to travel and see a lot for a country boy. I enjoyed seeing each and every country and hope I learned something from each of the countries.

While writing this, it feels like I'm there all over again. If I were young again, I would do it all over again, and I would do it the same way. The joy that it brought to me and the friendships along the way will be in my heart for a long time—actually, forever. The parties, the people, the sights, the events in life—and shared with friends and most important, my wife. She just made everything more enjoyable for me.

The two months that President Kennedy cut off of my tour made the time get real close to going home. I left Germany in October. I left Helga behind, because she wanted to see her brother off to the German Army. This was just after Christmas. She left Germany on her birthday and arrived on January 7, 1963.

When I got to McGuire Air Force Base in New Jersey, I wanted the time to go fast so I could go on home. It did not work that way. They put all of us who were coming back in a temporary barracks. About sixteen of us were getting out. They were behind in their processing because so many were getting out because of the cutback. They came by and told us to go and police a huge area. We did, and this went on every day. We picked up paper, went to eat, and went back to picking up paper. Finally after the first week, I got tired of the runaround and went and sat down. The airman first class told me to get to picking up paper. I told him that I had followed every order for four years now and I was getting out of the military. I told him that I was not going to pick the paper up. The other airmen agreed with me that this did not make any sense and that it was showing disrespect to each airman after serving his time. This was work for the basic trainees, not us. The airman first class agreed with us but said he would get in trouble. I told him to keep moving from one place to another and take a break each time at the new place and everything would be okay. We agreed, and it worked out for the next four days.

Then the processing started up again. Finally I finished with the processing. I was a free man and had a pocket full of money. The money was mustering-out pay. I had saved up fifty-three days of leave time.

Six of us airmen went to a little bar just outside the base in a little town where there was a bus station. We walked in, and the bartender asked everyone what they wanted to drink. When he got to me, he asked for an ID card—that brought a laugh from everyone. This was the first time I used the ID card for age, and it felt good.

Soon it was time for the bus, and I caught it. I was going to see my older brother, who was still in Maryland. I would ride the bus to Salisberry, Maryland, and meet up with him. We visited for three days. I told my brother if he would take me to the other side of town and let me off, I was going to thumb my way home. My brother pointed the way to the Chesapeake Bay Bridge. I caught three rides to the edge of the bridge. Then a car came along, and it was a Thunderbird Ford. This brought up memories because I had packed the drag chutes for the Thunderbirds and the Blue Angels while in Germany. They are the ones who put on the air shows for special occasions.

This would be the longest thumbing trip of my life. As close as I could figure, it would be about 807 miles long. I rode in the Thunderbird all the way to the other side of Copper Hill, Tennessee. The driver was a traveling salesman and was going back to his home on the edge of Tennessee. The tires were as slick as a peeled onion. This did not worry the man a bit. He said, "I will get a set of tires put on when I get home, not before." This made me feel uneasy, but there was nothing I could do.

I reached for my bag and asked at the same time, "Want a drink?" The driver accepted, and we drank and talked and drank and talked until the bottle was empty. It was brandy and low in alcohol, but had a good taste. Since it was late October, this knocked the chill off. I pulled out another bottle and we took a drink of it. I said, "I'm getting hungry, and I'll buy."

"I won't hear of it," said the salesman.

We ate steak and I drank coffee, remembering where I had learned to like coffee. I cleared my mind of it; *I'll have time, later, to remember.*

The salesman dropped me off and pointed the way to the truck stop. He said, "When you get to the truck stop, this highway will take you to Cleveland, Tennessee."

While at the truck stop, I ate breakfast and asked the waitress if she would find out who was going to Nashville, Tennessee—that I needed a ride. She came back and told me, "See that man over there? He said you could have a ride. Wait on him to get through with his breakfast and be ready to go."

I rode on his truck, his *slow* truck that was overloaded with chickens, loaded even out over the hood. It stank, and the two drivers had not had a bath either. We made it to Manchester, Tennessee, and I was only eleven miles from my hometown. I'd had about all I could take for a day and over half of the night. I called a cab—I was going home.

The cab let me out at the old house, and I went through the front door, still unlocked like before. I went to the hall closet and got a blanket and a pillow and lay down on the couch. I was already asleep when I heard my name called out. "Fred, is that you?"

"Yes," I answered.

Dad hugged me and ran down the hall, calling to my mom, "Guess who is home?"

Mom said, "I knew it," and jumped up.

Dad said she had been sick for the last few days. But she was over the sickness now, and we talked and talked. I finally said, "I'll have to catch up later. I need a nap."

I went around to visit everyone that I was close to, and my grandma was first on my list. I rested up a couple days and then went off job hunting. I found a used car and let my dad have his car back.

I could not find a job anywhere. I went to the employment office and checked them out. They said I did not have enough credits to draw unemployment and they did not have a place to send me to look for work.

I finally found work at a car lot washing and cleaning cars and lining them up on the lot. I did a little bit of everything. It did not pay good, but it would keep my mind occupied. Then I went to Genesco Shoe Factory and got a job that started at six o'clock at night and ended at two thirty in the early morning hours. I went home to sleep until seven o'clock and then went back to work at the car lot. I worked on Saturday mornings too.

Helga came over from Germany, and my sisters loved her. I was sure happy to see her. The long trip had worn her out.

I got an upstairs apartment, and we moved into it. It was real close to Genesco, and I could walk to work and come home for lunch. I quit the car lot, which was on the other side of town, and went to work at the car lot just down the road one street over.

At the shoe factory I worked in the cutting department, which involved cutting parts of shoes out of leather. This job ran short of work, and my boss did not want to lay me off. He invented a cleanup job. He told me to keep coming in at the same time and clean up the fans in his department. The hand sewing department started up, and I was transferred to that department. I had worked the night shift all winter long. I did not like the night shift and it was nasty work, so I was glad of the transfer. I was a hand sewer of shoes now.

I had been in this department for three months when my daughter was born. I was a proud father, and Genesco let me off for three days. When I got back on the job, they presented me with the Proud Pop Award. The baby was a girl, and she had dark hair like her mother. I was standing in front of the viewing window, and the fathers and grandparents were looking at the babies. A woman pointed at my baby and said she looked like a little rat with the long dark hair. I got on the grandmother and chewed her out for calling my baby a rat. She apologized and said she had meant nothing by the comment.

I went on working at Genesco. I was on the day shift now. I learned how to sew real fast and reached production level within the first thirteen weeks. When they needed an instructor, my boss asked me to take the job. The job was straight pay and more money than just working production—and I was not going to have to work as hard day in and day out. I like teaching and helping people. The other instructors and the boss gave the people they thought could not make it to me. I knew what was going on, and I accepted the responsibility and the challenge. I told each hand sewer when I got them not to let me down and we would make it together. I had 100 percent of the people the other instructors passed on to me meeting the production quotas.

The year went by real fast, and my daughter was getting prettier all the time. I was wondering what the next baby would be, a boy or a girl. The time arrived, and to the hospital we went. It was a boy. He was a good-looking little fellow. I was happy that both children were born healthy and with good looks.

I was showing my son one day to an old man that worked for Genesco. When Mr. Willie saw my boy, he started to laugh and said, "That baby looks just like me."

I said, "No, he does not," and it was getting my blood up a little.

Mr. Willie said, "Look at him real close, and you will see he looks just like me."

"No, he does not," I repeated.

Mr. Willie said, "He does. The baby has a bald head and he doesn't have any teeth, and I don't either."

We laughed and laughed about it. Every time I saw Mr. Willie after that, I would say, "No, he does not," and we would laugh again.

But I wanted something different. I know people that worked all their lives at factories and had nothing to show for their efforts except a living. I wanted more for my family and for myself. Not just a mere living. I did not want to be like my father and mother. Existing was the name of the game for them, nothing for the future. I wanted more out of life, and I started looking for another job.

Then I got a job with Fuller Brush. The sales business lasted five weeks. I was real good and made big bucks, and the boss begged me to stay. He offered me any area I wanted, but I knew this was not for me.

I got a job with Thrift Loan Co., and this was better. They told me I was an assistant manager. This was a dress-up job, the tie and white shirt kind. The pay was more than the factory, and it was easier work. I was an insurance writer for auto insurance, fire, theft, and collision. This was long hours, and I worked half a day on Saturdays.

Chapter 29

I Remember

I went by and told my mom about the new job, and we got to talking. The brother just younger than me was working on the golf course with my dad. My older brother was in Maryland, and now I was in my own place and had a family.

Then a memory came up. I said, "Do you remember the razor strap? It was about four feet long, a hole in one end for hanging it up, four inches wide, made of thick harness leather, with seven little fingers on the end."

Mom said yes.

"Mom, do you remember when my younger brother had hid the strap to keep from getting it used on him. Dad was looking for the strap to whip him with it and the strap could not be found. Dad offered a quarter to anyone who found the strap. A short while went by and here came my brother with the strap."

Dad said, "where did you find the strap?" My brother showed my dad how it was in a bush weaved in and out, so it was hard to see.

You know it, he got the whipping and did not get the quarter.

"And, Mom, do you remember the time you had my next-younger brother and I stay out of school and do the wash? And my brother had gotten in the habit when you called him to do something of saying, 'Salute you, captain.' He picked this up from watching *The Three Stooges* on TV. The day I'm talking about was when my brother went off and left me to do the washing by myself. I called on you to make him come back and get to work. When you called him to come, he jumped to attention and said, 'Salute you, captain.' After the second time, you told him that if he said that anymore, you were going to hit him in the mouth. He went off, hiding to get out of work again, and I called on you once more to get him back on the job. When he came in to the kitchen and popped to attention saying, 'Salute you, captain,' you slapped him in the mouth real hard. He jumped back grabbing his mouth and saying, 'A man can't say anything around here without getting hit in the mouth.' And, Mom, you finally told him if he left again that you would get the strap out. You said, 'I will not call you anymore. You stay and help your brother with the wash. It was well worth the aggravation to see this happen. It was so funny."

Mom and I laughed about it once more.

This picture is of six children in family. Bottom Row – Right to Left is my oldest Brother. I'm the one in the middle. We live through the hard times and all of the children are still living and going on with our lives.

And then I said, "Mom, do you remember when I brought the stray dog in the bathroom and was putting the used motor oil and sulfur mix on the dog for the mange? It got all over the bathroom, and you were mad. I carried the dog outside and turned him loose. I forget how the bathroom got cleaned up. I think I paid my sisters to clean up the bathroom."

Mom and I laughed about that story too. Then I asked her, "Mom, you were mad that day, were you not?" and we laughed again.

Then I asked her, "Remember the dog next door, and how the man would get drunk and beat the dog? This went on for a while. Then I was coming home late at night from the bowling alley, and I helped the dog out. I released him and off he went, and the owner never did find the dog. The old man moved, and I was just thinking good riddance."

I left my mom's house and was going to my house, feeling good thinking about this. Then my mind went to one thing and then to another, on and on.

I remembered that every Thursday my mom would wash, and one of us kids had to stay home and help her do the wash. My next-younger brother and I were swapping out every other week. It came my time, and I explained to my mom that I had a test at school and I needed to take the test in order to graduate from high school. Mom said, "You are staying at home and doing the wash." I refused and went to school. I told my mom I was not going to fail for anyone or any reason. Mom stayed mad, and I never did the wash again that I remember. Mom always told me, "You g-- da-- little devil, you won't live to be twenty-one years old." I've heard that ever since the wristwatch incident in Maryland. The Lord and I have proved her wrong.

Then I remembered the liver. Mom and Dad liked liver at least twice a month. I could not stand to smell it cooking and would get sick and heave up if I tried to eat it. I asked Mom to

fix me something else, and she said, "Eat the liver or do without."
I did the latter. I had to hold my breath when I came home and
smelled liver cooking. I still can't eat liver, but it does not bother
me as much to smell it now.

I had to think of something funny and get my mind off this
stuff. Then I remembered when Charlie, the son of my adopted
grandma—the younger son, not the one in the air force—was
clowning around with white bread. He was putting the bread
in his mouth one slice after the other. Charlie would chew on
the bread and get it moist and pack it in each side of his mouth.
It made his jaws puff out wide, and he looked like a pack rat.
Charlie kept putting the slices in his mouth. Since he needed a
little help, I took the end of the table knife and packed the bread
a little tighter. Charlie ran around with the bread in his mouth
clowning and looking in the mirror and making all kinds of jests.
Charlie and I did not know that the bread would harden up after
awhile.

Finally Charlie wanted to get the bread out of his mouth,
but he couldn't and neither could I. Charlie's mouth was dry,
and he needed a drink. I ran to get help. I was small at the time,
but I found Grandma and she came running to see what was
going on. She said, "Why, Charlie,"—but then she just started
laughing. Charlie was trying to tell her that he could not get the
bread out.

I spoke up. I said, "Grandma, Charlie can't get the bread out,
and he needs a drink of water."

Grandma said, "You get it out the same way you put it in
there."

I got the knife and was getting the bread loose and out of
his mouth one little piece at a time. When his mouth was finally
empty, he got a drink and we started laughing. Then I noticed his
jaws had stretched out and were sagging, and we started laughing
again. I would remind Charlie of this every once in a while, and
we would laugh again. It might have been a world record if we
had kept count.

Then I was thinking about the time I learned to ride a bicycle. I was pedaling the bike around and around after a boy got me started off on the bicycle. I could hear everyone saying, "Keep your head up and look where you are going." I would hold my head up and then look right back down; I wanted to see the pedals and the wheel go round. I kept going around and around in a big circle, and then I came out of the circle and ran into the brick wall and crashed. I flew over the handlebars and headed on into the wall. I rolled over and asked what had happened. A group of kids from the neighborhood were watching. They started laughing, and the teasing began; they were mocking me. The kids had their heads down and were running around in circles and acting like they had crashed into the wall. All of this was funny, and we all enjoyed ourselves that day—at my expense.

Then I remembered the time we boys were picking up walnuts when we were in the third grade. My hands were stained from picking the green walnuts up and hulling them out. We would eat what we wanted and sell the rest. My hands were stained almost black, but I went off to school. I could not wash the stain off. The teacher asked and I explained about the walnut stain. She understood. Lunchtime came. We students all lined up, washed our hands, and were walked to the lunchroom. We were going through the line when I was stopped and was told to go wash my hands. I went and washed my hands and got in line again. The woman looked at my hands and told me to go wash my hands again. I explained that it was walnut stain and my hands were clean. The teacher came over and said, "That's the same story he told me, and I believe him." The woman still said, "Go wash your hands, or no lunch." So I was off to wash my hands again. When I got back to the lunchroom, the line was closed, and I did without lunch.

When I got home, I told my mom what had happened. She went to school with me the next day. I told her that the teacher had told the other woman that she believed me. My mom went straight to the lunchroom; I had not been to class yet. Mom asked for the woman in charge yesterday, and she came out. I told Mom that it was not her. Mom asked for the woman that told me to go wash my hands. I saw the woman in back; she did not want to come out. Mom told the woman in charge, "Go get her right now, or I will go get her myself." The woman came out, and Mom told her about the stain on my hands. Mom said, "If you ever again make my son go without eating his lunch or imply that his hands are not clean, I will come up here and kick your butt. Do you hear me, and do you understand what I'm saying to you?"

The woman nervously shook her hands and said, "I understand." Mom took me to the classroom, watched me go to my desk, nodded to the teacher, and was gone.

I think it was a lot better in the country schools, the old one-room schoolhouse. The country teachers understood the hard way of life—and when hands were dirty and when they were not dirty.

And then I remembered breaking the teacher's son's arm. Now that was a day. We lived on the old Robertson farm, and the teacher's name was Miss Roberson. Recess was on, and I was trying to join in on the games being played. Miss Roberson's son and four other boys got in a circle and started pushing me. One would shove me, and then another would shove me. I was trying to get out of the circle, but they would not let me. Shove after shove came, and they started calling me Fido, a dog's name. I had about all of this stuff that I was going to take, and something had to give.

I saw a tree limb laying on the ground and started making my way to it. The shoves were still coming, one way, then the other—and then I was over to the big tree limb. I picked the limb up real fast before they knew what was happening and brought it down hard toward the head of the first boy in line of the limb. It happened to be the son of Miss Roberson. He threw up his arm to stop the blow. He did stop the blow but not before it broke his arm and the limb broke in two. The boys scattered, and Miss Roberson's son was yelling, screaming, crying, and down on his knees. Then he was back up again, and holding his arm started to the schoolhouse; Miss Roberson was on her way to him. Miss Roberson knew it was broken. She put her son in the car and came to the classroom and rang the bell. She put the oldest kid in charge and was off to the doctor.

When they came back, her son had a cast on the arm. Miss Roberson came toward me. I was sitting at my desk. When she got to me, she slapped me upside of the head and I went flying out of the desk and to the floor. I asked Miss Roberson what that was for. "For breaking his arm," she said.

I said, "He caused it."

"What?"

Then a girl spoke up and told the story about the boys shoving me and calling me Fido. Several of the students said the same thing. Miss Roberson got on to her son for not telling the whole story, and then she apologized to me. "I'm sorry for not checking it out," she said Miss Roberson drove us kids home that afternoon and apologized to Mom and Dad.

Dad said, "That is okay; he needed it anyway."

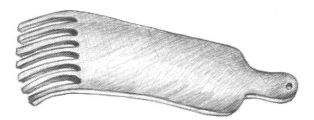

This strap did its job well. All of the children are law abiding citizens and God fearing people.

When we kids were going to Unionville School the following year, just before school started Miss Roberson came to our house and asked us to change schools. She said they were going to close the school down if more kids did not sign up to go. Miss Roberson said, "I will send the bus after you right here in front of the house."

We changed schools. We were going back to the old school. I was sitting in the class doing work, and this boy sitting behind me kept leaning forward and talking about the clothes I wore. Grady was from Walking Horse people, who had money and dressed in dress pants and white shirts most of the time. I called Miss Roberson over and told her what Grady was saying to me about the pants. I told her that if he said it again, I would pop him in the mouth. Miss Roberson said, "You have my permission."

I knew this was a green light for me. Recess was on, and we started to play tag. I was It until I tagged a fast boy by accident. I told him to tag Grady. He was off around the trees and then around the schoolhouse. I knew that Grady would run close to the building to round the corners off. I ran over to the corner of the schoolhouse and put my eye where I could see around the corner. I waited on Grady to come. When he came, I was ready. I stuck out my little arm with my fist on the end of it. He never saw it coming. Pop—and blood was coming from his mouth. He was holding his mouth and crying. I stood over him saying, "I told you to keep your mouth shut," while I was pointing my finger at him.

Grady went and told Miss Roberson that I had hit him in the mouth. Miss Roberson said, "That is good; you got what was coming to you. And he had my permission. Grady, go and clean the blood off your mouth and get back in your desk." My teacher just smiled at me and went back to teaching.

Chapter 30

New Job Looking For Better

This new job was working out real well. The pay was good, but the hours were long. I found out about a house trailer that was for sale by taking over the payments. It was ten feet wide by sixty feet long, the biggest back in those days. We needed the room, so I bought the trailer.

I was still looking for a better job. One day I was talking to a linen truck driver, who said his company was looking for a driver to start work in the Nashville area. I headed to Nashville, checked this out, and got the job. I worked in Nashville during the week and came home on weekends while training was going on. They assigned me to a McMinnville route, and I had the house trailer pulled to McMinnville, our new home. Then I moved up the ladder and became an extra route man, and we moved to Madison, Tennessee. The next move was to Pegram, Tennessee. The moves were all easy; we just packed the dishes, taped all the cabinet doors, and pulled the house trailer away. I went into supervision and stayed there two years. Then I was promoted to service manager and stayed there over five years until I quit. In total I had stayed with the linen company for over eleven years.

I got a job with UPS and started delivering packages. Then I went to the over–the-road trucks, and I finally found a home of a job. The pay was good, and the work not bad. I could hold out on this job and do the work really well until I could retire. I would be able to raise my two children and provide for them and my wife with no problems. The insurance was good, and I had the weekend off for quality time with the family.

I sold the house trailer when I became the service manager. We bought a house in Ashland, Tennessee. We lived there for twenty-one years and sold the house after we built the dream home that we live in now. I drew up the plans and designed the home; Helga had input as well. We researched log homes for five years. I forgot to tell you that I took mechanical drawing in school. I'm sure glad I did; it saved six hundred dollars on the blueprints.

I changed jobs seven times after I left high school. Each time I changed jobs, I bettered myself. I loved the linen company work and hated to leave, but big companies think they own you for life once you are in management. The bosses think you will not leave, and this leads to long hours and less pay and less respect. The UPS driving job turned out good, but my wife and I didn't like the hours I was working—half nights and half days. It was the best I could get because of seniority. I could take in my two children's ballgames by missing two hours of sleep or by breaking my sleep up. I missed a lot of the games, but I tried to see as many as I could. My wife and I enjoyed seeing the children gain confidence in their abilities and grow while having a good time.

Our children took on responsibilities and grew into adults very quickly. Both children were honor students going through high school. Neither child caused any trouble. They both are very fine people, and my wife and I have had so many compliments about them we cannot start to count them. No dope, no smoking, no cussing, not lazy one bit, not overweight, and they will have a social drink from time to time but not too often. My wife and

I are very proud of our children. We thank them for being good children.

I know there is no jealousy between the two. I have always taught them that I loved them the same. Whatever money I spent on one child, I spent on the other. They got the same amount of money for Christmas presents, birthdays, graduation, or whatever. They were taught from an early age that we, their mom and dad, loved them the same.

This was not possible in the home where I grew up. I can see the results of it from time to time, from one conversation to another. My home was different, and we broke the cycle by raising our children right.

I told both of our children that if I ever heard either child say that I or their mom treated the other better than they were treated, that I would hit them in the mouth.

Chapter 31

Retirement

I worked twenty-five years with UPS, and it was good times and a lot of laughs. The company was good, and the pay was okay too. There were a few rough spots here and there, but for the most part it was enjoyable. A few supervisors were not up to snuff; the light was on, but no one was at home. They should have never been in supervision. I look at supervision as though it is a teaching position, instead of a disciplinary position. A lot of good people worked for the company. The good times we had and the laughs on the CB radio kept us going in the night, keeping us awake and alert. I went by Cotton Top for my CB "handle," my name while talking on the radio.

In my twenty-five years with this company, I drove more than eighty times around the world in a Mack truck. I had no chargeable accidents. I was recognized for my service and driving skills. I got far more than the watch that everyone talks about when retiring. I'm retired now and have been for almost seven years. I mow a lot of grass and take care of my place. Out of twenty-eight acres, I have about eight of those acres to mow. I love shooting skeet, trap, and sporting clays, and I have a three-stand trap here on the place. I shoot at Willows Sporting Clays in Tunic, Mississippi, when my wife and I go down there.

I had open-heart surgery almost two years ago. Then I had a pacemaker put in, and I have been doing fine since. I exercise almost every day, walk a lot, and stick to my diet. I thank the Lord almost every day that he let me live, and I'm enjoying every minute. I have no doubts about there being guardian angels sent to watch over me. I thank the Lord for letting St. Thomas Hospital be here and for guiding me to the hospital.

Almost everyone that I was friends with said, "You will not like retirement as much as you think you will." Those friends are now saying, "I'm going to retire and enjoy it, like you are." I tell them it's whatever one makes of it. I tell them to find a hobby, like skeet, bowling, or something they like to do on a regular basic. I also tell them to include their wife, and there will be more to do and more to talk about.

Chapter 32

Reasons Why I Think as I Do

I was not a problem child and fighting because I liked it. Stop and think: I lived at nineteen different places up to the time I got out of high school. New schools twice a year in many of the years. The bullies always found the smallest to pick on. I was taught to take up for myself at an early age. I was whipped at home, and sometimes I thought I should not have had a whipping. I was not going to take a whipping at school and not fight back. Most of the time, it only took one fight when I changed schools; and the bullies knew I was little but I would fight back. Then we all got along just fine.

When I started to grow in the last year of high school, things started to turn around for me. I grew two inches in the last year and filled out with some pounds. The better food that I was getting made the difference. I was in control of my own money, and if hungry I could buy something to eat; I had never eaten a hamburger until I bought myself one. We never ate beef that I can remember while growing up. The meat we ate was hog, groundhog, possum, squirrel, rabbit, chicken, fish, and turtles. The two inches in height made a big difference, believe me.

I told you that I was a rock-throwing champion. Well, here is another incident that will back me up. I was outside next to the road and had my pockets full of rocks. A big older boy from three streets over rode up on his bicycle. He was talking about the rocks I had in my pockets, asking questions such as, "Are you good at throwing the rocks?"

My answer was, "I think I'm real good."

He said, "See that electric meter over there on the end of the house? I bet you a nickel that you can't hit that meter three times in a row."

I said, "I won't bet that way, but I will bet three times out of five."

He handed me a big rock that he picked up off the ground. Then I knew what he wanted me to do. He wanted me to break the electric meter glass and get in trouble. I repeated the bet, three out of five. I threw rocks that were small and almost round. I was two out of four and had to hit with the last rock to win the bet. The big boy was smiling and trying to make small talk so I would miss. He knew that I was not going to break the glass. I threw the rock and hit the meter. The smile stopped, and he got mad and said it was just luck. He put his foot on the pedal of the bicycle and started to push off without paying me. I told him if he did not pay the nickel that I would rock him. "When you are trying to leave and get up speed on the bicycle to outrun me, I can hit you with rocks at least ten times or better. Your back and your head are big targets for me to hit."

His foot came to the ground, and he paid me the nickel. He rode off with his head hanging down after a glance back at the electric meter. The big thing was I *had* to hit the meter because I did not have a nickel to pay if I missed. I was proud of myself and looked at the nickel as I was walking toward the house. Then I declared myself the National Champion Rock Thrower of all times. I won while being under pressure. This felt good.

Mom was almost blind as a child of about nine years old. The measles had settled in her eyes. She slowly came out of it and could see pretty good. Mom had to wear glasses to read when in her fifties. Mom's mother died at a young age, and Mom was the one to take care of the family and finish raising the siblings. She did all of the cooking and washing dishes and clothes. She mended the clothes and did all the household chores while Grandpa and the older two boys were farming. This was a hardship on a young girl.

When Dad came along, Mom fell in love, deep down like an oil well a mile deep. She never did come to the top for air. She loved so much she was blind to everything around her, including her children. She thought her children were like her siblings, and there was not much love to give after raising her siblings. Mom wanted everything for our dad at any cost to make him happy. Mom was there to please and would give up her children to please our dad. Mom and Dad always got the best piece of meat, no matter what we were eating. They always had their coffee and cigarettes. My favorite piece of the chicken was the neck. It was mine, and no one else wanted it. It was there even if I was late getting to the table. My mother had a rough life and was making her life worse all the time. My older brother and I tried several times through the years to get Mom to not take Dad back after one of his episodes, but Mom would not listen. Mom loved Dad so much she did not love herself or her children.

Mom has never said "I'm sorry" for anything or admitted to anything about the hard times. She still thinks that her children owe her something for the life that we have. Mom was jealous about everything and everyone around her. She could never wish good for anyone. We had to please Dad, or my mom was mad. Mom would always say bad things like, "I hope you go to jail. I hope you lose all of that money, You won't live to be twenty-one years old. You will be sorry. What goes around comes around." All of the siblings and I have talked about it several times; we have forgiven them and still have love for them. How, I don't know, but we do. I don't ever remember any time that our mom or dad picked one of us children up in their arms and consoled us. Neither does my sister.

Our father was a strange dude. Both of his parents died when he was very young. He lived wherever he wanted, with his sister, brother, or his aunts and other relatives. He hoboed around from town to town and state to state. He told us he had been in thirty-two states by age thirteen. My father was telling one of his adventures of being on the road. He said he was hungry and broke. He went up to a house and knocked, and a woman came to the door. He asked, "Can I do some work for a meal?"

She stood there for a minute and then said, "Yes, you can split up some kindling. Go around back, and I'll show you what to do." In back of the house was an old shed. She rolled out a big barrel and said, "See the pile of boards? I want you to cut those boards into kindling. The barrel has to be full before you are to eat."

My dad said okay, and she left. He picked up the old ax, and it was dull. He said, "I'm hungry. I have to split the kindling if I am going to get something to eat." He started busting and chopping the kindling, and the longer he worked the duller the ax became. Then a idea came to mind. He started making noise like he was splitting the kindling. When he thought the meal would be ready, he flipped the barrel upside down and piled the kindling on the bottom of the barrel. He had enough split to cover the bottom real good, and he kept making noise like he was working. The woman came to the door and said, "My, you split kindling real fast, don't you?"

"Yes, ma'am, I sure do."

"Come and get your meal. There is a pan of water on the back porch to wash up."

Dad said he ate it all up; it was good and it filled him full. He thanked the woman, and he was off. He said, "I walked real fast because at any time she might discover that she had been beat at her own game."

My dad learned to live from day to day. He did not want anything more than he could carry around, any more than he could load up in a old pickup truck and haul off and be gone. Sometimes he would work real hard, and he would have us and Mom convinced that he was going to do the right thing. He would have us thinking, *This is the way it should be*, and the way was better for everyone. We as a family would have all the bills paid and have an old car and some new shoes and coveralls on; our bellies were full, and everything was looking up. Dad would round up every cent he could and say, "I'm going to get seeds and stuff to plant. I'll be back." Then Dad would go borrow money on the mules or farm or just lie about the collateral and get him some more money to blow.

Dad would gamble at cards and pool games. He was not good at either game. When he came home, he would be broke and acted like he was sorry; Mom would always take him back. The big potato crop that brought over four thousand dollars disappeared as fast as the four and five hundred dollar trips. The old car that he left in broke down, blew up, and was not worth fixing. After five days of his being gone, Mom heard some noise in the fruit cellar. Mom got Uncle Robert, and they went to see what the noise was; it was our dad hiding in the fruit cellar. Dad said he was trying to sober up. Mom said he said he had been there in the cellar for two days. Dad told my mom that he was eating potatoes and canned peaches and fruit right out of the cans.

I know that neither of the parents loved us children when we were young. When we got older, I think Dad learned to love us, but Mom never did. Dad and I talked about it one time. He said, "The hard times I put all of you through—are you holding it against me? Do you think I was too hard on you children?"

I said, "Yes, it was hard, very hard; but if it was too much, we would be dead, and we would not be talking about it now."

My dad said, "I think I taught all of my kids how to work and not to be afraid of work."

I said, "Yes, you did that all right." I really think he was trying to apologize, but did not know how to say it and still be in control. I told my dad that I had no quarrels about anything and what was in the past would stay in the past. My dad's time was close, and he did not know it. Dad had heart trouble for ten years. He had to carry the little nitro pill everywhere with him. Dad did not quit and sit down completely. Dad kept trying to make a dollar at something. The change came when all the children were grown—but it was too little too late. The last thing he said to my mom was, "I love you and the kids." Then he turned and went to bed. He had a massive heart attack that night and died.

Out of all the hard times for the six children—hunger, and being poorly dressed, cold, overworked, and undereducated— goodness still had a way to get through. I can say that for what we came through, all six of us are doing well and enjoying life; we all thank the Lord for pulling us through.

My story is just one of six living through this kind of upbringing. There are no bad eggs in the children. There are no drugs, no jail time, and no alcoholics among us kids. It seems that we all were born with common sense. There are only seven grandchildren out of the six children. We all learned, "If you can't feed, clothe, shelter, and educate kids, do not get them." We were all born with responsibility and common sense.

We learned not to give up when trying to do something. We learned that hard work will not kill your children, that it makes children stronger and wiser. When children get the paycheck and learn how hard it was to make, it only takes a little while for them to learn how to handle money. You parents out there, don't be afraid to let your children work, but let the children keep what they earn. I know you have heard the old saying, "I want my children to have it easier than I had it." If every generation gains 10 percent of this goal, in ten generations the problem will be solved. When a child is born and named, write his name on a retirement account. This way he will get a check monthly and will retire shortly after he pops into the world. This child will not have to go to school or work or do anything in his whole life. As soon as he is grown, let him buy his own house and move out on his own. This is the way to help your grandchildren.

Chapter 33

Being Conservative

All of us siblings knew to work for what we wanted and for what we needed. We did not need the government or depend on others for help. I grew up being a conservative even though I did not know what it meant. I know now and still can't get away from being conservative. I have tried to be wasteful, but can't. I have found out I can enjoy life without being wasteful. I do not waste food. I try to never take out more than I can eat. I do not eat and eat to get my money's worth. I do not buy unless I'm going to use it, unless it's an investment. I'm not greedy. I have always taken the sure way, not the fast way, to prosperity. I do not gamble big time, only for small-time entertainment. I compare prices three times before I buy a big item and research the item before I buy it. These are some of the rules I go by in being a conservative.

This is a poem I wrote; I hope you enjoy it.

I'm Conservative

I'm a conservative, for I am debt-free,
Proud to be a conservative for I will never go on a spending spree.
I'm not here to put on a show;
When it comes to spending money I'm always slow.

So, I'm proud to be a conservative and live in the land of
      the free.

I'm a worker, busy as a honeybee.
Take me as a conservative or forever let me be.
Let us all pay as we go. That will be cash,
We will have money left over for the corned beef hash.

So, I'm proud to be a conservative and live in the land of
      the free.

When the job is done, just holler;
I will pay in cash dollars.
Do not depend on future pay raises for vacations and play,
Because if it does not happen it's hell to pay.

So, I'm proud to be a conservative and live in the land of
      the free.

Off your butts, onto your feet,
Get out of the shade into the heat.
If you don't work, you don't eat.
Being a conservative cannot be beat.

So, I'm proud to be a conservative and live in the land of
      the free.

We should not ever use the plastic card,
Paying back interest rates could be very hard.

I'm a conservative inside and out,
With happiness bubbling over, here comes a shout.

So, I'm proud to be a conservative and live in the land of
the free.

Wake up Americans. Being a conservative is not bad,
Waking up in a free America can be had.

I'm a conservative and proud to be. If the Lord is willing, I
will always be debt-free.
I'm happy to be in a free America, with no one sending
overdue bills to me.
I'm proud to be a conservative in the land of the free.

By Fred W. Campbell

Along the way, I learned some things in picking people or
friends that I wanted to be around.

Mouth Open or Closed?

Knowledge acquired, if not passed on, is forgotten and will
be of no value to anyone.
Teach what you have learned, and help someone without the
use of money.
Very quiet people are of no value, not even to themselves.
People that like to be spoken to, but will not speak to others
first, are selfish, confused, lazy individuals.
Very quiet people are confused and are hiding things from
other people and themselves.
Very loud people are looking for attention and can be teachers
if the necessary knowledge is acquired.
People who say very little have little to contribute to the
conversation.

Loud people know when to be quiet. That is, when you have
    a quiet person talking.
Loud people have more fun because more of them are blonds.
Quiet people do not listen. If they listened, they would know
    and have something to talk about.

These sayings help to define the type of person you have just met.
After reading them a few times, you will get a laugh when you recognize a
person in one of these quotes. You may understand your friends better.

A thought just ran through my head. It's about Mac, the dog. I
remember how Mac would knock on the door to get into the house.
There was one time when he was really muddy all over. Mac came to
the door and knocked. Mom went to the door and looked out. Mom
could not see anyone, so she stepped out on the porch for a look down
the street. When Mom opened the door, Mac slipped through, went
straight to the bedroom, jumped up on the bed, and laid his head on
the pillow and fell asleep. Mom saw the mud all over the floor and
followed the footprints to the bedroom. Mom saw Mac sleeping with
his head still on the pillow. Mom got a broom and slammed it down
on the bed, making a loud pop. Mac woke up and ran through the
house and behind the couch to hide. Mac would not come out until
the kids came home. Mac didn't trust my mom anymore after that.
When Mac knocked on the door to be let in, Mom would let him in
and he would go behind the couch until it was safe.
    Mom often told the story. We kids petted the dog and talked to
him. We all thought it was funny and had laughs from it and teased
our mom about having to clean it up. Mac did not think it was funny,
though, because he did not get on the bed anymore.

The H-words are a part of life. Without the H-words being in your
life your life is not complete. This is only my way of thinking. This
means you have been sheltered too much and smothered too much;
you have had too much help from others.

Happiness is a way of life. It makes everything you do easier and more enjoyable. When you are happy, that means everyone around you will be happy. Surround yourself with happiness.

Humor is when you have happiness in what you are trying to accomplish in life.

Heart is when you try and try again when you get knocked down; just keep getting back up.

Most people say *hate* is a bad thing. Hate is a good thing if used properly. It gives you strength. Hate stops you from being lazy. If you hate to be hungry, you won't have time to be lazy. Use hate to your advantage. Hate develops when you have to do something you don't like over and over again.

Hunger is when you have no food. Hunger is when you want better and you have a plan. You can have hunger for a lot of things. You can satisfy your hunger with honesty and hard work, along with having faith of doing the right thing.

Honesty is what keeps you in line to accomplish all of those things in your plans.

Holiness is when you have faith and are thankful to the Lord for giving you the strength to thank him, the Lord, and be grateful for what you have accomplished in life.

These are the seven H-words to have in your life. If you are like I am, without these words, you have the feeling that something is missing. I think you have to have them all to be complete.

I know what you are thinking. What about the other H-word, the hell word? Hell happens all the time when going through life. Hell is lurking in the shadows all the time.

Live the other H-words, and hell will be of no importance to you.

Live them:

Happiness

Humor

Heart

Hate

Hunger

Honesty

Holiness

Chapter 34

New Challenges

My wife and I are getting close to our fifty-year anniversary. We are living in our dream home, a log house. We are trying to eat healthy and exercise. We go to Tunic, Mississippi, for two and three days at a time. A mini vacation, every six to eight weeks.

I'm learning the computer. It's a challenge for me. I can ask questions until I'm blue in the face, and most people that are computer wizards cannot answer the questions. They can show you, but they cannot tell you. I said I didn't want a computer in my house, but I have two of them. My wife and I have two computers set up with games and slot machines. We have a little competition and see who can do the best; it's fun and passes the time very well. I've started reading again and have read ten books in the past year. The books are of the learning kind, and a novel from time to time with a mystery thrown in occasionally.

My younger sister inspired me to write this book, the stories of my life. She said when she told some of her friends some of the stories, they would not believe them. My sister said, "There are six different stories here. All of the six are success stories."

I've always wanted to write, but did not know what to write about.

My sister said, "Write about you. You know what happened to you."

I wrote some political papers and a poem.

I've told the stories from the way I remember them. I left out several events. I did not want my parents looking too bad. And I did not want to get sued for making your hair come out. You would not believe some of the stories. I'm going to leave the rest for your imagination.

I've written mostly about my older brother and my next-younger brother. I know some of the stories about the three youngest siblings, but I was not there when they happened. We three oldest were always working. We would work, eat, sleep, and go to school when we could. So maybe my sister will write the story about the three youngest siblings that are not mentioned very much in this book.

In the summer months, my wife and I sit on the deck and drink coffee, taking in a few sun rays. My wife's parents were not up to snuff either. They took her money and gave her an allowance until she was twenty-one years old. My wife was still living at home and staying with her grandma. So when she and I talk, we can relate to one another about growing-up pains.

Who is to second-guess all of this? If this had not happened, what would have happened? I would have been this or that or even greater. I could have been a multimillionaire or even richer. Look at it from a different angle. I could have been as bad as my parents were or even worse. I could have been in jail, a bum, a murderer, or whatever. Who knows?

Too much money makes one greedy. Money puts stress and worry on its owner. How am I going to keep it? How am I going to make some more money? With my heart problem, I do not need this. I will not second-guess any part of my life. I will just be very happy the way it's turned out. I would not want to change anything in my life. I lived through hard times. I'm enjoying my retirement years to the fullest. Who is to say the hard times did me harm? I know they made me stronger and a better person.

I know I had some rough edges to wear off. I've worked on the rough edges over the years and have smoothed them out. I think everything worked out well for the family members. Growing up like I did gave me an advantage of knowing what not to do. I knew that I would never take a penny from my family and not pay it back. I knew that I would not hold my children hostage and make slaves out of them. I knew that it was up to me to provide for my family. I had two jobs several different times in my life.

Let me give you an example of how much discipline I had toward all the money made that went into the family pot. I started a knife collection. In order for me to add to my collection, I would order a dozen knives. I put one of those knives in my collection. I would sell the other eleven to make the money to pay for the knives, including the one in my collection. The older I got, the less love I had for the knives. I sold the entire collection except for the knives that were my Dad's. I used this system on other things as my interests changed and went on to other things. I'm comfortable with what I got.

My purpose in life was to make a good home for my family and be able to retire without being dependent on my children, the government, or anyone. With help from my wife, we succeeded. Now we are enjoying life at a slower pace, and we are pleased. There are no clocks to punch in and out, and no one to tell me to hit the floor and build the fire at four in the morning. I have chores to do for my wife, but they are enjoyable. We wait on phone calls once a week from our children. If they don't call on schedule, we call them. Life is great. If the Lord is willing, we hope to be around for our seventieth wedding anniversary. That is only about twenty years away from now.

From my experience love is not always a great thing. When someone tells you that too much love can destroy and tear down everything built up in a family, believe them it's true. Two parents can love each other so strongly that there is no love left for the children. Too much love for one another restricts them from saying no to one another.

In the same way, some mothers love their children too much and won't turn them loose to make their own way. Mothers can be their children's worst enemy when it comes time to grow up. I freed myself at age nineteen. I have not looked back, except for memories and a look back to see what I did not want to do. That was for self-guidance.

If you think that you have had it rough, hard, or whatever, hop in my shoes for the first nineteen years. I will guarantee you the rest of your life will be a walk along oceanfront beaches of your choice. I've wondered several times during my life, when we siblings get to talking about the strap that was used on us, where it is now. The strap that had seven little fingers on it. I'm hoping the bush that it was hidden in is still hiding it.

While writing this book, I thought about the woman with the kindling barrel. I've been wondering if her eyes and screams were as big as Airman Miller's were. The incident with the cat crawling down deep under the covers, and the screams of torture that came out for everyone to hear. Did the woman cuss my dad? I'm betting she did. If it was my mom, I know the choice words she would use on him.